TAKING THE COMPLEXITY
OUT OF
CONCEPTS

TANIA LATTANZIO & ANDREA MULLER

WITH NICOLE GINNANE

ALIGNED TO THE
AUSTRALIAN CURRICULUM

Taking the Complexity Out of Concepts

This book is available at special discounts when purchased in quantity for use as premiums, promotions, fundraisers, or for educational purposes. For inquiries and details, contact the publisher: info@elevatebooksedu.com.

Published by Elevate Books EDU

Del Mar, California

Library of Congress Control Number: On File

Paperback ISBN: 979-8-9851374-9-1

CONTENTS

INTRODUCTION

ABOUT INNOVATIVE GLOBAL EDUCATION

INNOVATIVEGLOBALED.ORG

Innovative Global Education (IGE) is a professional learning provider that delivers a range of professional learning services to schools and educators across the globe. The aim of IGE is to facilitate creative, practical and flexible solutions that build capacity for sustainable educational innovation and development.

At IGE, one of our primary areas of expertise is curriculum and instructional development with a focus on conceptual learning and inquiry. In this capacity, we have repeatedly been requested to support principals and teachers who are challenged with managing the shift from a content-based curriculum to one driven by concepts and conceptual understandings. Each time, the underlying issues have been the same: firstly, the absence of a clear approach to developing a framework for conceptual learning, and, secondly, a lack of understanding about how the framework will translate into classroom practice. Further, the educators with whom we have collaborated had found it difficult to locate useful resources offering practical solutions and strategies for dealing with these issues.

To meet the demand for better professional learning materials focused on conceptual learning, IGE has created a set of tools to guide conceptual curriculum design. Having trialled a number of processes for developing conceptual understandings, we selected the most workable of these techniques and integrated them into a comprehensive framework: the IGE Model for Formulating Conceptual Understandings, presented in Chapter 2 of this book. Given that we are ourselves practitioners, each aspect of the framework is based in our own educational experience in working towards understanding conceptual learning alongside our fellow educators.

We have facilitated the IGE Model for Formulating Conceptual Understandings in countries across the world; with principals, coordinators and teachers of every subject and year level; and in reference to a range of national and international curriculums. As a result of this work, we have been privileged to witness firsthand how the resource has been received by educators. We have found that the model is quickly understood and applied by principals, team leaders and teachers alike, resulting in shared clarification and understanding within teaching teams. Educators who work with IGE consistently remark on how effectively the model strips away the mystery of conceptual understanding: 'That was so much easier! Why has no-one ever told us that before?'

Although the IGE Model for Formulating Conceptual Understandings was an immediate success, we noticed that educators still struggled to design effective and engaging conceptual lessons and assessments. IGE has developed a planning tool, the IGE Template for Planning Conceptual Learning (see Chapter 5, pp. 53–80), that supports educators to plan their lessons using a conceptual approach and assess student mastery through a rubric of understanding for conceptual assessment (see Chapter 4, pp. 47–52). Our models draw together the various aspects of the IGE approach to provide a comprehensive tool that takes teachers from conceptual theory to classroom practice.

Now that educators have access to tools that support the design of conceptual curriculum and conceptual teaching and learning, they feel more informed and confident and about developing conceptual units. In making the IGE framework available through this book, we hope that many more principals, teachers and other educational professionals will be able to avoid the complexities and harness the many benefits of conceptual learning.

CONCEPTUAL LEARNING AND THE AUSTRALIAN CURRICULUM

Although the IGE approach to conceptual learning can be used with any state, national or international curriculum, the standards used in this book come from the Australian Curriculum. The Australian Curriculum, like many national curriculums, has an excess of content. A recent review endorsed 'the widely held view that overcrowding – too much content – is the most serious problem with the current Australian Curriculum' and highlighted 'a design weakness observable from the beginning: the absence of an overarching framework' (Adoniou et al. 2014).

Although IGE is not in the business of critiquing the Australian Curriculum, we do aim to provide educators with a method for translating content into concepts. Teachers don't have the time to continually rewrite the curriculum, but they do need to be clear about the purpose of the content that they teach. While the Australian Curriculum can certainly be taught in terms of conceptual understandings that lead to greater coherency and purpose, a teacher with limited knowledge of concepts would struggle to identify these conceptual elements. The IGE approach strengthens teachers' ability to identify conceptual understandings and enables them to meet curriculum requirements within a conceptual mode of learning that is compelling, significant and intriguing for students.

Further evidence of the need to reimagine the Australian Curriculum in terms of concepts is the increasing number of schools in Australia implementing the International Baccalaureate (IB), particularly the Primary Years Programme (PYP) and Middle Years Programme (MYP). Both PYP and MYP have an explicit emphasis on conceptual learning that stems from the formulation of central ideas and statements of inquiry – called 'conceptual understandings' in the IGE framework. For the growing number of educators who are required to teach the Australian Curriculum through an IB framework, the IGE Model for Formulating Conceptual Understandings offers a uniquely efficient way to develop the central ideas and statements of inquiry required for teaching PYP and MYP. Although this book has been used in connection to the Australian Curriculum, please note all examples can be applied to any national and/or International curriculum. It is the process that is the most important factor.

HOW TO USE THIS BOOK

Taking the Complexity out of Concepts is intended as a practical resource that will assist educators with the pedagogical shift from a content-based curriculum to a conceptual curriculum. It is, in other words, a handbook on how to plan, teach and assess conceptually. As authors, our aim is to do just what the title suggests: take the complexity out of concepts in learning by providing practical strategies and ideas that can be implemented in any setting.

Although this book is structured as a resource for educators, it is crucial that students are given the chance to build their own awareness of the role of conceptual understanding in their learning. Teachers have frequently stated to us that explicit teaching of the instructional strategies documented in *Taking the Complexity out of Concepts* improves learning outcomes for students, yet research tells us that metacognitive learning strategies are infrequently explained to students (Askell-Williams 2014). IGE therefore strongly recommends that teachers take the time to instruct their students on what concepts are, how they work and why they are important; to guide discussions about conceptual understandings; and to support the development of each learner's individual conceptual framework. Without an understanding of what concepts are and how they work, the learner's success in developing conceptual understandings can be limited. By contrast, an awareness of the conceptual learning process positions students as masters of their own learning, helping them to deliberately leverage the neural pathways that enable the effective acquisition, classification and retrieval of concepts.

IGE believes that within a conceptual approach to learning, the educator's role is first and foremost to connect learners with the concept. Teachers can capture their students' attention and ignite their curiosity by taking excursions, engaging with experts, sharing stories and creating artworks – to name but a few possible approaches. What matters is that the process of learning is initiated by provoking the learner's desire to make meaning. Teachers can then encourage students to independently evaluate new knowledge and develop their own ideas.

In this book, IGE provides a number of case studies that teachers can use to guide them when employing the IGE tools for conceptual learning. Each case study is adapted from IGE's professional learning work with schools and includes examples of how educators are using the models in their classrooms (some case studies have been modified to ensure consistency with the requirements of the book). Where applicable, we have offered some recollections about the background to each case study.

To conclude, we ask readers to please take note of two points. First, in this book as in our IGE practice, we use the term 'conceptual understanding'. In other educational settings and programs, conceptual understandings may be referred to by synonyms including 'enduring understandings', 'central ideas', 'big ideas' or 'statements of inquiry'. And second, it is important to note that as with all educational practice, our work is constantly changing as we reflect, review and strive to meet the needs of our fellow practitioners. The models and other resources presented in this book have gone through many changes, and we have no doubt they will continue to do so.

CHAPTER OUTLINE

↘ **Chapter 1** provides the definition of a concept, distinguishes between disciplinary and interdisciplinary concepts and explains the benefits of conceptual learning. It also outlines the research that informs conceptual learning and thinking, focusing particularly on the work of educational psychologist Jerome Bruner and the 1970s American humanities program Man: A Course of Study (MACOS).

↘ **Chapter 2** introduces the IGE Model for Formulating Conceptual Understandings, which has been used successfully by educators around the world as a step-by-step process to develop conceptual understandings. The chapter also provides examples of the model in practice, all of which are adapted from units devised by IGE in collaboration with practitioners.

↘ **Chapter 3** looks at the process of inquiry in relation to conceptual learning. At IGE, we believe strongly that the success in conceptual learning is directly linked to teaching through inquiry. Rather than viewing inquiry as step-by-step procedure, we advocate for inquiry as a process into which all elements of the inquiry process have been incorporated.

↘ **Chapter 4** describes how to plan appropriate assessments connected to conceptual learning. By modelling the development of a rubric for the assessment conceptual understanding, the chapter aims to equip educators with tools necessary to develop relevant assessments that connect to the understanding goals and overarching conceptual understanding.

↘ **Chapter 5** presents the IGE Template for Planning Conceptual Learning. This planning template has been developed to help educators ensure that conceptual understandings are at the forefront of lesson design. Five examples of the model in practice are given as a foundation upon which educators may build.

CHAPTER 1:
THE WHAT AND WHY OF CONCEPTUAL LEARNING

We might ask, as a criterion for any subject taught in primary school, whether, when fully developed, it is worth an adult's knowing, and whether having known it as a child makes a person a better adult. If the answer to both questions is negative or ambiguous, then the material is cluttering the curriculum.

— Jerome Bruner (1960, p. 52)

WHAT IS A CONCEPT?

According to H Lynn Erickson (2008, p. 30), a concept is 'a mental construct that is timeless, universal, and abstract.' In the world of education, a concept acts as an umbrella, linking together all the details and characteristics that form the constituent parts of that idea. Because they reveal the relationship between seemingly discrete pieces of knowledge, concepts enable learners to organise and scaffold their learning and thinking in a way that is directed towards stronger understanding. A concept can typically be expressed in a single word or a phrase, such as power or points of view.

Traditionally, educators have taught through content as opposed to concepts. In this context, content is defined as discrete pieces of factual information that can be observed and verified. When students memorise the capital cities of Europe, the dates of key events in World War II or the names of Australia's native animals, they are learning through content.

Yet while factual information is important, it does not guarantee that learners will draw on this knowledge use it and apply the content in meaningful ways. Kip Téllez (n.d.) points out that while 'facts are crucial to overall knowledge development', when taken alone they 'do not generalize well. They are specific to the context in which they are taught'. But factual content can also be taught through a conceptual framework, which emphasises both depth and breadth of understanding.

Table 1.1 illustrates the contrasting attributes of content and concepts.

CONTENT IS ...	CONCEPTS ARE ...
• concrete • narrow • specific • limited • verifiable • observable	• abstract • broad • universal • timeless • applicable in different contexts • represented by many different examples

Table 1.1   Differences between content and concepts
Adapted from Erickson (2007, 2008)

In a recent IGE workshop, one teacher posed an instructive question: 'Why isn't a table a concept? After all, a table is not just one thing: it can be any number of sizes, styles and materials.' In this example, the teacher was viewing a table as an observable, concrete object, not as an abstract concept. But 'table' can also be broad, abstract and applicable in different contexts – think of a table of contents, table of thought, table of ideas and so on.

Here's a quick self-assessment exercise to test your understanding. How would you describe each of the words in Table 1.2? Are they content or concepts? See the opposite page to check your answers.

WORD	CONCEPT OR CONTENT?	WORD	CONCEPT OR CONTENT?
symbols		levels	
systems		exploration	
Shanghai		house	
process		paper	
mountain		weather	
dog		time	
collaboration		clothes	
instruments		structure	
style		dinosaur	
density		flow	

Table 1.2   Concept or content?

The following are concepts:

- symbols
- collaboration
- style
- levels
- systems
- process

- density
- exploration
- time
- flow
- structure

The following are not concepts:

- Shanghai
- mountain
- house
- weather
- clothes

- dinosaur
- dog
- instruments
- paper

How did you go?

DISCIPLINARY AND INTERDISCIPLINARY CONCEPTS

In disciplinary teaching, learning takes place within a single subject, and understandings are presented only in the specific terms of that subject. By contrast, when teaching in an interdisciplinary mode, the aim is to incorporate a number of subjects by examining understandings across a range of disciplines. In a unit that is interdisciplinary, learning occurs through exploration of the connections between disciplines.

Concepts themselves can be either disciplinary or interdisciplinary. Table 1.3 outlines the respective characteristics of disciplinary and interdisciplinary concepts.

DISCIPLINARY CONCEPTS	INTERDISCIPLINARY CONCEPTS
<ul><li>usually studied within a single discipline</li><li>narrower than interdisciplinary concepts</li><li>enable depth and complexity in disciplinary teaching</li><li>provide a focus for planning, teaching and learning within a discipline</li><li>aim to develop disciplinary competence rather than broad facts and skills</li></ul>	<ul><li>span across two or more disciplines</li><li>broader than disciplinary concepts</li><li>provide opportunities for connection across the curriculum</li><li>provide access to depth and complexity to allow for conceptual understanding</li><li>can be revisited and spiralled throughout the curriculum to scaffold learning</li></ul>

Table 1.3   Differences between disciplinary and interdisciplinary concepts

Table 1.4 presents some examples of disciplinary concepts organised by learning area.

Science	Mathematics
• velocity • genetics • matter	• computation • differential • equation
Civics and citizenship • civilisation • governance • market	**English** • characterisation • genre • convention
Health and physical education • attack and defence • health • body form	**Visual arts** • colour • tone • texture

Table 1.4   Examples of disciplinary concepts

Table 1.5 shows some examples of interdisciplinary concepts that span across learning areas.

PATTERNS	SYSTEMS	POWER
Mathematics • patterns in algebra • patterns in geometry	**Science** • ecosystems • planetary systems	**Civics and citizenship** • power of government
Science • patterns in life cycles	**History** • social systems	**English** • power in literary texts
English • patterns in poetry	**Economics and business** • business systems	**Health and physical education** • power in movement
Visual arts • patterns in artworks	**Mathematics** • number systems	**Science** • energy as power
Music • patterns in rhythm • patterns in composition	**Digital technologies** • information systems • software systems	

Table 1.5   Examples of interdisciplinary concepts

Although some concepts are necessarily specific to one discipline, conceptual learning can be more effective when it incorporates interdisciplinary concepts as well. Benefits of using interdisciplinary concepts include the following:

↘ **The focus remains on the concept, not the subject.** In an interdisciplinary mode of learning, students focus on fundamental concepts, and subject-area content and skills are taught through a conceptual lens. Although the specifics of instruction may vary due to the distinctive ways in which a particular concept manifests within different subjects, students will come to recognise the conceptual links between subjects in a way that reinforces, challenges and extends their understanding.

↘ **The cognitive process of seeing patterns and connections is activated at the conceptual level of thinking.** In contrast to a fragmentary mode of understanding in which learning begins anew with each subject, students begin to see the patterns and connections across subjects that make learning meaningful and purposeful.

↘ **Planning, teaching and assessment of the concept are integrated across subjects and year levels.** For educators, interdisciplinary teaching of concepts encourages collaboration and promotes schoolwide consistency and coherence of instruction.

THE HISTORY OF CONCEPTUAL LEARNING

PIAGET'S THEORY OF COGNITIVE SCHEMAS

At the heart of IGE's practice of conceptual learning is a psychological construct known as a schema. Simply put, a schema is a mental structure that enables us to make sense of our knowledge, understandings, thoughts and experiences. Think of it as a cognitive filing system, designed to help you store, organise and retrieve the many disparate pieces of information that reside in your brain. Each schema is unique to the individual who creates it, since each learner has their own methods for organising, reviewing, adapting, developing and interacting with information.

The idea that schemas are a key element of our capacity to learn has roots in the writings of developmental psychologist Jean Piaget (1928), whose work led him to the realisation that knowledge is dynamic and cumulative rather than static or discrete. In other words, learning is as much about building on a learner's current understandings – their existing cognitive schemas – as it is about the development of new understandings. According to Piaget, schemas are the mental scaffoldings that make possible the categorisation, processing and recollection of information – yet these scaffoldings are not fixed but instead adaptable in response to new experiences. For example, a child who owns a pet goldfish may have a schema in which all fish are orange-coloured, live in water and breathe through their gills. When the child visits a friend and is shown a tank full of tropical fish, that child must adapt their schema to account for the new knowledge that fish can be many different colours. Here, a schema has enabled the child to identify links with their existing knowledge and thus generate new knowledge about what a fish is and how to recognise one. When learning occurs through schemas, it is the connections between items of information that are the essential drivers of learning.

Given what we know about the way in which schemas support understanding, it is easy to see the significance of Piaget's theory for contemporary educators; indeed, it would be reasonable to assume that the majority of teachers are already utilising this powerful cognitive tool in their classrooms. Surprisingly, however, recent research suggests that the potential benefits of brain-based teaching and learning are not widely recognised by educators in either the United States or Australia (Askell-Williams 2014; Dunlosky 2013). At IGE, we believe that a shift from content-based to conceptual instruction will ensure that schemas becomes an explicit aspect of instructional practice. Because our approach is built upon the neural connections that link facts together in the form of concepts, it differs from content-driven instruction by leveraging the full potential of brain schemas in the service of improved learning outcomes.

BRUNER AND THE SPIRAL CURRICULUM

Piaget's writing on schemas had a significant influence on the educational psychologist Jerome Bruner, whose work set forth the theory of learning as concept attainment. In *A Study of Thinking*, Bruner, Jacqueline Goodnow and George Austin (2009) argue that understanding is guided by the capacity of the learner to compare and contrast items of information based on their various attributes. Recalling Piaget's schemas, Bruner and his colleagues explain concepts as the mental categories that we use to classify information according to its common features.

In his follow-up to *A Study of Thinking*, entitled *The Process of Education*, Bruner (1960) sets out to solve the problem of "how to have the basic subjects rewritten and their teaching materials revamped in such a way that the pervading and powerful ideas and attitudes relating to them are given a central role" (p. 18). In response to this issue, he puts forward the influential notion of the spiral curriculum, whereby key ideas are first introduced to children in simplified form and then revisited in progressively more advanced ways. For Bruner, the underlying rationale of such a curriculum is that learning should reflect what is most important within society: 'A curriculum ought to be built around the great issues, principles, and values that a society deems worthy of the continual concern of its members' (p. 52). Consequently, spiral curriculum begins by 'tempting' the child – sparking their curiosity about ideas that are important to understand and worthy of investigation. By revisiting these ideas over a period of time, learners are able to deepen their understanding of an idea and explore it in a range of different contexts.

Within the spiral curriculum, learning is not compartmentalised into discrete subjects with their own attached knowledge and skills. Rather, the design of school curriculum hinges on ideas of importance that are worth knowing, exploring and re-exploring over a sustained period of time. Through an emphasis on the big ideas, fundamental principles and foundational beliefs that have importance, longevity and are meaningful to humans, Bruner's method enables educators to de-clutter the school curriculum. IGE's models for curriculum and planning owe a clear debt to Bruner's notion of the spiral curriculum and its emphasis on the cumulative step-by-step build-up of conceptual understandings.

MAN: A COURSE OF STUDY

Man: A Course of Study (MACOS) was a humanities program developed in the United States in the late 1960s and popular in a number of countries – including Australia – during the 1970s. The program, which was based on Bruner's theory of the spiral curriculum, was designed to teach a single concept – that of the 'lifeline', or the entire history of a living being. Students were progressively introduced first to the simple life cycle of a salmon, then to the more complex lifespans of herring gulls and baboons, and finally to the lifetime of a human through a case study of the Netsilik Inuit people. This learning was supported by a kit of inventive primary resources, including films, games and visual aids, with which students were encouraged to engage using a variety of disciplinary strategies. Teachers of MACOS were expected to play a significant role in engaging students with the course, since the success of the course was believed to depend upon the teacher's success in building this engagement.

MACOS was a progressive and intellectually rigorous program, but it was highly controversial. It was eventually abandoned after a concerted campaign of opposition that focused on the cross-cultural nature of the course materials and its emphasis on a secular society. But in subsequent years, research on MACOS showed the following benefits:

- ⭘ **Students demonstrated interest, curiosity and engagement in their learning.** They felt genuine interest in learning about lifetimes and what it meant to be human, that this was important for humanity.

- ⭘ **Students worked interdependently and showed high levels of collaboration.** The authors described this as reciprocal learning, creating a community of learners. Their inquiries were collaborative and created with a shared sense of purpose.

- ⭘ **Vocabulary competence increased by 30 per cent.** By exposing the students to rich language they were able to effectively acquire a more complex vocabulary related to their conceptual inquiries. The meta-language of each subject was used as experts would use it. There was no sense of using simple language; rather, rich vocabulary was used. We see this in our work with students, providing accurate, complex vocabulary allows the learner to think like an expert and truly access the disciplinary knowledge that they need to explore complexity.

- ⭘ **Students from low socioeconomic areas gained as much conceptual mastery as others.** Conceptual learning allows teachers to start with the experiences and existing knowledge of their students enabling all students to connect and develop their understandings.

- ⭘ **Less-able students benefitted from scaffolding.** The students who were more able preferred to start with the concept and to explore it from a 'big picture' approach. Less able students benefitted from being introduced to the concept and then having scaffolding to help them understand the steps to understanding.

- ⭘ **MACOS educators adopted the role of 'researcher of learning'.** They used data and observations of learning throughout the investigation, steering the students towards understanding and monitoring the learning process. In MACOS, the concepts were introduced by the teacher and explored in depth through a process of inquiry. Driving concepts included the complexity of life and the lifespans of living organisms. The course was centred on the conceptual question 'What makes man human?' The teacher used resources as a provocation to learning, which engaged the curiosity of the students and led to further exploration. It was certainly a highly engaging and sequential program that enabled students to better understand what it means to be human.

Despite its untimely demise, MACOS remains a clearly articulated model for concept-based learning that incorporates comprehensive planning and support material. As such, it has had considerable influence on IGE's updated approach to conceptual learning. For readers who want to learn about MACOS in more detail, we recommend www.macosonline.org, which makes available for non-commercial use a variety of materials from the original initiative. Those interested in unpacking the controversy surrounding MACOS may wish to seek out the documentary *Through These Eyes* (2004), which looks at both the development of the program and the controversy that led to its abandonment.

CONCEPTUAL LEARNING IN THE 21st CENTURY

In the wake of 20th-century theorists like Piaget and Bruner, educators today continue to explore conceptual learning. Erickson (2007, 2008), one of the foremost contemporary experts on conceptual learning design, has been influential in the development of the concept-based International Baccalaureate PYP and MYP programs. In *Concept-Based Curriculum and Instruction: Teaching Beyond the Facts*, Erickson makes a strong argument for the importance of introducing concepts to students in the earliest years of schooling:

> *Trying to teach in the 21st century without a conceptual schema for knowledge is like trying to build a house without a blueprint. Where do the pieces go? It is too late to wait until high school and college to 'dump' key concepts and conceptual ideas on students. Conceptual development is a lifelong developmental process. Conceptual understanding requires a higher-level, integrative thinking ability that needs to be taught systematically through all levels of schooling. Integrated thinking is the ability to insightfully draw patterns and connections between related facts, ideas, and examples, and to synthesize information at a conceptual level.* (Erickson 2007, p. 8)

While Erickson's work focuses on how conceptual learning can enhance curriculum and planning, New Zealand educator Mark Treadwell (2008) has taken a different perspective by exploring neuroscience behind conceptual learning. Treadwell illuminates the way in which the brain constructs schemas, showing how the process of adding to and reviewing schemas over time enables the ability to apply concepts in new and innovative ways. The brain schema in this way becomes a foundation from which conceptual thinking can emerge. By introducing students to a concept, establishing what they know and then consciously building on their understanding, conceptual learning can improve long-term retention and application of ideas. Thus, Treadwell concludes that 'introducing new work based on concepts, and ensuring that the learner has reflected on their present understanding of the concept, provides a far stronger basis for iteratively improving their present model of understanding, removing misinformation along the way' (p. 251).

21st-century researchers like Erickson and Treadwell have made valuable contributions to the body of evidence that supports a conceptual approach to learning. But IGE had found that many practitioners still lack the tools to incorporate concepts into their day-to-day practice. This book is an attempt to fulfil that need by providing teachers with easy-to-use models that will enable them to conveniently translate content into concepts and plan lessons using a conceptual framework.

THE BENEFITS OF CONCEPTUAL LEARNING

When prompting teachers to think about why we teach through concepts, IGE often shows a short YouTube clip entitled 'Are our children learning enough about whales?' (2008), produced by satirical media organisation *The Onion*. This humorous video, in which a panel of teachers express their outrage that 'only 84% of education funding goes to teaching children about whales', emphasises the fact that in education, we often attempt to teach content to students despite having no clear sense of why it is important for them to learn. Why do we need to study whales? How will knowing about whales help students to make sense of their world?

Frequently, the educators who attend our workshops respond to the video from *The Onion* with their own examples of topics they have taught or experienced as a student without consideration for the purpose and meaning of the learning. During a recent session, one teacher mentioned that Year 4 students at her school were taught a unit on electricity and magnetism. Yet when we questioned the group about what made this unit significant and compelling – Why are the students learning about these two topics? How are electricity and magnetism connected? What is the underlying big idea? – the teachers could not answer. They kept talking about electricity as circuits and magnetism as magnets, but they struggled to come up with an overarching rationale for the unit.

When even teachers have no grasp of why the curriculum prescribes the content it does, it should be no surprise that some students cannot see the purpose of the learning. If teachers were able to position curriculum content within an overarching conceptual framework, this would give a context for the facts and potentially provide students with a compelling reason for learning. The IGE approach to conceptual learning encourages educators to ask themselves, 'Why are the students learning about this topic? Is it relevant to their lives? For example, rather than memorising types of whales and their characteristics, students could inquire into the topic of whales through the concepts of extinction or ecosystems. Students can still find out all about whales, but now they have a clear rationale and coherent framework guiding their exploration.

In the case of the teachers struggling to justify a unit on electricity and magnetism, we are not saying that these scientific ideas are not important; in the lower primary years, but they might be more effectively taught as a unit with a focus on the concept of materials in which students could explore a variety of materials and how they work. In upper primary years, students could be shown how electricity and magnetism relate to the concepts of forces, energy and sustainability. Again, students will be exposed to critical knowledge about electricity and magnetism, and they will also be able to link the key facts about electricity and magnets through their understanding of relevant concepts.

Another example is that of the secondary school teacher struggling to devise a heavily knowledge-based history unit for her Year 9 students. The teacher had spent hours collecting information – she literally had folders full of it! – and showed real dedication to the subject, but her thinking about how much content had to be explicitly taught was guided by the notion of coverage. But when she began using the IGE model, the teacher's focus immediately shifted from content coverage to understanding. She realised that for her students, it was not the content in itself but rather the concepts of progress and continuity that caught their interest, as they could see the relevance of these ideas reflected in their own lives.

It is important to recognise that making the transition to a conceptual curriculum does not require you to throw out your current units and start again from scratch. It is likely that your existing units have the potential to be taught conceptually once you have the tools to do so. But if you cannot identify the significance of the unit or the big idea from a conceptual perspective, the topic might not be worth exploring. To assist you in this process, Table 1.6 presents a checklist to help teachers decide if the units they currently teach have the potential to be taught conceptually. This resource is available for download at **go.hbe.com.au**.

CRITERIA FOR DECIDING ON UNITS	YES	NO
Is the unit compelling? Is it of interest and relevance to the students?		
Is the unit significant? Are there connections to the learner's real world?		
Is the unit intriguing? Will it produce learning engagements that capture students' attention and curiosity?		
Is the unit purposeful? Is it about something that is worth knowing?		
Are students provided with opportunities to transfer and apply their learning? Now that they have understood the understanding goals what can they do with it?		
Is the unit comprehensive? Is there enough complexity to ensure that students spend their time in meaningful inquiry?		
Is the unit conceptual? Is it focused on learning about big ideas of importance rather than disconnected facts?		

Table 1.6   Criteria for deciding on units

IGE recognises the importance of facts, knowledge and skills. But we strongly believe that without a conceptual framework, students' ability to retain and connect learning is compromised. IGE's approach to conceptual learning supports students to create and maintain the cognitive schemas that allow them to organise, retrieve and connect new and existing knowledge. Research indicates that one of the benefits of learning through concepts is that 'organizing information into a conceptual framework allows for greater "transfer"; that is, it allows the student to apply what was learned in new situations and to learn related information more quickly' (Bransford, Brown & Cocking 2000, p. 17). By leveraging the way in which the brain processes information, conceptual learning contextualises curriculum content and makes it meaningful. It creates genuine interest by engaging students in learning that is relevant to their lives and their world.

The examples in Table 1.7 have been developed as a way to get teachers thinking about how to make the shift from content to concepts. This process is further outlined in the following chapter, in which the IGE Model for Developing Conceptual Understandings is introduced to assist educators in creating their own conceptual understandings.

CONTENT	CONCEPTS
dinosaurs	extinction, adaptation, cause and effect
geometry	relationships, design, measurement
world wars	conflict, causality, power
friends	relationships, friendship, belonging
plants	growth, needs, habitat
weather	cycles, patterns, systems
Ancient Rome	civilisation, development, technology

Table 1.7　Shifting from content to concepts

CHAPTER 2: FORMULATING CONCEPTUAL UNDERSTANDINGS

THE IGE MODEL FOR FORMULATING CONCEPTUAL UNDERSTANDINGS

In the course of IGE's past work with schools and educators, we noticed that many teachers were struggling to understand how to convert a unit of instruction from a content-driven unit to a conceptual unit. Although many schools demanded that teachers use concepts in lesson planning, few provided clear guidelines about the process for doing so. The following statement is a summary of reflections that teachers have voiced to us in team planning sessions:

> *When we came to plan our units, we discovered that we had to identify 2–3 concepts for each unit. The ones we chose kind of seemed to make sense with what we were intending to teach, but we really only looked for concepts at all because there was a section on the unit plan where we had to record them. We did not consider whether our concepts were significant or compelling. As we began to use the IGE model, we realised that we had been concentrating on content instead of using concepts to structure meaningful inquiry.*

It was clear to us that just like the teacher in this story, many educators were spending considerable time on identifying concepts, yet their efforts were ultimately misguided because they lacked a structured process for conceptual analysis. The IGE Model for Formulating Conceptual Understandings (Table 2.1, p. 18) has been created in response to this challenge. It enables educators to translate curriculum content into concepts that deepen subject-specific understanding while providing opportunities for connections across the curriculum. The IGE model ensures a level of conceptual clarity that teachers have previously struggled to achieve. Since introducing the model in workshop sessions, we have received overwhelmingly positive feedback that is summarised in the comment below:

> *In the past, it has taken us so many collaborative planning meetings to try and sort out the conceptual focus for our units. We now realise that we were doing the process backwards, selecting a big idea without really knowing where it came from. Now that we use the IGE model, it is so much easier to reach a consensus about what we want the students to understand conceptually.*

STEP 5: CONCEPTUAL UNDERSTANDING How can the understanding goals be written as a single statement?	
STEP 4: CONCEPTS What concepts are the focus for the unit?	
STEP 3: UNDERSTANDING GOALS What 3–4 things should students understand by the end of the unit? *Students will understand …*	
STEP 2: ASK Why is the unit compelling? Why is the unit significant? Why is the unit intriguing?	
STEP 1: CONTENT What is the content to be explored in the unit?	

Table 2.1   IGE Model for Formulating Conceptual Understandings

What the IGE model provides is a structured process that guides teacher dialogue with the aim of identifying understanding goals, extracting concepts from within these goals and then developing a conceptual understanding. A blank version of the model is available for download at **go.hbe.com.au**.

HOW TO USE THE IGE MODEL FOR FORMULATING CONCEPTUAL UNDERSTANDINGS

In this section, we provide a detailed run-down of how to complete each step of the model in order to highlight the conceptual elements within curriculum content. The process should conclude with the development of an overarching conceptual understanding that drives teaching and learning.

At the commencement of a unit of instruction, students can be presented with the concepts, understanding goals and conceptual understanding that have been developed using the IGE Model for Formulating Conceptual Understandings. If students are particularly well-versed in conceptual learning practice, teachers may even like to solicit their input when completing the steps of the model.

STEP 1: CONTENT

The first step of the IGE Model for Formulating Conceptual Understandings is to identify the curriculum content that will be the starting point for conceptual understanding. When completing this step of the model, educators should list the standards, objectives and descriptors that they wish to cover in the unit.

Each of the five case studies for this chapter is based on a single content description from the Australian Curriculum. But the model works equally well with any mandated curriculum requirements or other school-designed curriculum. For examples of conceptual understanding that incorporate content descriptions from across the Australian Curriculum, see the case studies included in Chapter 5 of this book (pp. 53–80) to demonstrate the IGE Template for Planning Conceptual Learning.

STEP 2: PURPOSE

Before the conceptual understanding for a unit can be established, the following questions are vital. Their aim is to determine the value and purpose of the learning, as this will guide the development of understanding goals, concepts and finally the conceptual understanding.

> ↘ **Why is the unit compelling?** Compelling refers to the level of interest the unit has for the students who will be learning it. This question asks teachers to think about the 'why' for learners by looking at it through the eyes of the student. Why would a student be interested in learning about this?

↘ **Why is the unit significant?** Significant refers to the way in which the unit relates to a learner's real world, both now and in the future. What aspects of the unit are most relevant for students to learn? What real-world connections will they employ to make sense of their learning, and how will the learning help them to make sense of the world around them?

↘ **Why is the unit intriguing?** Intriguing refers to the potential for meaningful inquiry. This question assesses whether or not the unit has the potential to generate learning engagements that capture the learner's attention and build upon their previous understandings.

STEP 3: UNDERSTANDING GOALS

According to Tina Blythe and Associates (1998, p. 36), understanding goals 'are the concepts, processes, and skills that we most want our students to understand. They help to create focus by stating where students are going'. Step 3 of the IGE Model for Formulating Conceptual Understandings asks teachers to come up with 3–4 understanding goals that explain what their students are expected to understand by the end of the unit.

Understanding goals should be derived from the body of knowledge identified in Step 1, but they are meant to highlight the aspects of the prescribed content that are most compelling, significant and intriguing for learners. The teacher's purpose in developing understanding goals is not to state what a student should know or be able to do, but rather what they will understand; thus, we recommend that teachers use the sentence starter, 'Students will understand …' We have also found it useful to rephrase the understanding goals as questions, as switching back and forth between questions and statements can bring additional clarity (Blythe & Associates 1998).

When teachers are working collaboratively towards conceptual learning, the cooperative development of understanding goals ensures a common direction for the conceptual elements of the unit. The goals can be used to guide consistent and authentic formative and summative assessment (see Chapter 4, pp. 47–52). Table 2.2 is a checklist to assist in the development of understanding goals. It is available for download at **go.hbe.com.au**.

CHECKLIST FOR STEP 3: UNDERSTANDING GOALS	YES	NO
Do the understanding goals relate to the content?		
Are the understanding goals clearly written and easy to understand?		
Are concepts implicit in the understanding goals?		
Do the understanding goals reflect the purpose of the unit?		
Are the understanding goals assessable?		

Table 2.2   Checklist for Step 3: Understanding goals

STEP 4: CONCEPTS

Concepts are single words or phrases that represent the big, abstract ideas that underpin a unit. Teachers should always select concepts with a clear connection to one or more of the understanding goals from Step 3. The concepts selected may be subject-specific, or they may be interdisciplinary. The selected concepts are central to informing the conceptual understanding in Step 5.

When selecting concepts as a team, it is important that there is a shared understanding as to the meaning of the concepts in the context of the learning. In a recent IGE planning session with teachers, the teachers commented that they wanted students to understand what the concepts of beliefs and values meant. But when the teachers were asked what they themselves thought these concepts meant, it was apparent that they did not have a shared understanding of the concepts. Through considerable discussion, debate and research, the teachers developed a collective understanding. This collective understanding ensures there is consistency of conceptual planning and teaching throughout the unit.

STEP 5: CONCEPTUAL UNDERSTANDING

A conceptual understanding is a broad statement that brings together the understanding goals identified in Step 3. It is written as a single sentence, and it includes most or all of the selected concepts from Step 4. Conceptual understandings are complex and have global significance, meaning that they have relevance for teaching and learning in a variety of contexts and conditions.

In Table 2.3, teachers will find a checklist to help them formulate conceptual understandings. This resource can be downloaded at **go.hbe.com.au**.

CHECKLIST FOR STEP 5: CONCEPTUAL UNDERSTANDING	YES	NO
Are most or all of the selected concepts included in the statement?		
Does the statement encompass most or all of the understanding goals?		
Is the statement written as a sentence?		
Is the statement broad and transferable?		
Is the statement written in a way that allows for complexity?		
Is the statement of interest to the students being taught?		

Table 2.3   Checklist for Step 5: Conceptual understanding

CASE STUDIES OF THE IGE MODEL FOR FORMULATING CONCEPTUAL UNDERSTANDINGS

These case studies show the development of each stage and how the model has been used in schools with educators. Each case study is based on IGE's work with real educators, although they have been condensed and edited for the purposes of this book.

CASE STUDY 1
SCIENCE UNIT
YEAR 4

SETTING THE SCENE

Most curriculums, including the Australian Curriculum, stipulate that students will learn about forces and motion at some stage in their primary years. But educators who must develop a unit connected to forces and motion are often challenged when it comes to making the unit conceptually compelling, significant and relevant. One of the questions teachers frequently ask is, 'How can we make this content accessible and authentic for students?' Once they have identified concepts and a conceptual understanding to guide the unit, teachers begin to think of real-life examples that give the unit relevance and meaning.

INTERDISCIPLINARY LINKS

There is a clear connection with the concept of forces in this content description from the Australian Curriculum: Design and Technologies.

↘ Australian Curriculum: Design and Technologies for Years 3 and 4

 • Investigate how forces and the properties of materials affect the behaviour of a product or system (ACTDEK011)

↘ Australian Curriculum: Health and Physical Education for Years 3 and 4

 • Practise and apply movement concepts and strategies with and without equipment (ACPMP045)

 • Combine elements of effort, space, time, objects and people when performing movement sequences (ACPMP047)

STEP 5: CONCEPTUAL UNDERSTANDING How can the understanding goals be written as a single statement?	Exploring the connection between forces and motion provides insight into their application in daily life.
STEP 4: CONCEPTS What concepts are the focus for the unit?	• forces • motion • variables • application
STEP 3: UNDERSTANDING GOALS What 3–4 ideas should students understand by the end of the unit?	Students will understand … • exploring the relationship between forces and motion • variables that affect motion • how we apply forces in our lives to create and/or innovate
STEP 2: ASK Why is the unit compelling? Why is the unit significant? Why is the unit intriguing?	• The unit is compelling because there is a direct connection between all movement and forces. • The unit is significant because forces are evident everywhere in our lives. • The unit is intriguing because changes in forces affect movement in ways that have application to our daily lives.
STEP 1: CONTENT What is the content to be explored in the unit?	Australian Curriculum: Science Year 4 • Forces can be exerted by one object on another through direct contact or from a distance (ACSSU076) 　• observing qualitatively how speed is affected by the size of a force 　• exploring how non-contact forces are similar to contact forces in terms of objects pushing and pulling another object 　• comparing and contrasting the effect of friction on different surfaces, such as tyres and shoes on a range of surfaces 　• investigating the effect of forces on the behaviour of an object through actions such as throwing, dropping, bouncing and rolling 　• exploring the forces of attraction and repulsion between magnets

Table 2.4　Case study 1: Science unit for Year 4

CASE STUDY 2
HEALTH AND PHYSICAL EDUCATION UNIT
YEARS 5 AND 6

SETTING THE SCENE

In reviewing the Australian Curriculum: Health and Physical Education for Years 5 and 6, it becomes apparent that there is a need for a unit that focuses on attack and defence in games.

Physical education teachers tend to approach curriculum content from the perspective of skill acquisition without considering the role of concepts. In working with the IGE model, these teachers soon realise that before students can achieve mastery of a given skill, they must develop a baseline of conceptual understanding. Most physical education teachers have not considered a conceptual approach before, and they are frequently surprised by the way in which clarifying what they want students to understand provides a more meaningful structure for the teaching of skills. As one teacher exclaimed, 'This gives so much purpose to the learning! I can see that for students, exploring the concepts first gives them a more authentic context for acquiring physical skills'.

INTERDISCIPLINARY LINKS

The concepts of space and movement recur repeatedly in the arts learning area of the Australian Curriculum. Here are three instances where connections between physical education and arts subjects could be established:

- ↘ Australian Curriculum: Drama for Years 5 and 6
  - Explore dramatic action, empathy and space in improvisations, playbuilding and scripted drama to develop characters and situations (ACADRM035)

- ↘ Australian Curriculum: Media Arts for Years 5 and 6
  - Develop skills with media technologies to shape space, time, movement and lighting within images, sounds and text (ACAMAM063)

- ↘ Australian Curriculum: Dance for Years 5 and 6
  - Perform dance using expressive skills to communicate a choreographer's ideas, including performing dances of cultural groups in the community (ACADAM011)

STEP 5: CONCEPTUAL UNDERSTANDING How can the understanding goals be written as a single statement?	Attack and defence in invasion games requires collaboration and effective use of space and movement.
STEP 4: CONCEPTS What concepts are the focus for the unit?	• attack and defence • collaboration • space • movement
STEP 3: UNDERSTANDING GOALS What 3–4 things should students understand by the end of the unit?	Students will understand … • the role of attack and defence in invasion games • how to effectively use space in invasion games • the role of movement in invasion games • how to work as a collaborative team
STEP 2: ASK Why is the unit compelling? Why is the unit significant? Why is the unit intriguing?	• The unit is compelling because utilising attack and defence requires an understanding of space, movement and team-building. • The unit is significant because attack and defence are significant skills in team sports. • The unit is intriguing because success in sports requires cooperation and teamwork.

STEP 1: CONTENT
 	
What is the content to be explored in the unit?
	Australian Curriculum: Health and Physical Education Years 5 and 6
	• Propose and apply movement concepts and strategies with and without equipment (ACPMP063)
	  • demonstrating defensive and offensive play in modified games
	  • proposing and applying movement concepts and strategies to perform movement sequences at different levels using different types of equipment
	  • proposing and applying movement concepts and strategies to safely traverse a natural environment

Table 2.5   Case study 2: Health and physical education unit for Years 5 and 6

CASE STUDY 3
INTERDISCIPLINARY UNIT
FOUNDATION YEAR

SETTING THE SCENE

When introducing concepts to early childhood teachers, we begin by focusing on how young children engage with the world around them. Most early childhood specialists recognise that young students learn through investigating and making discoveries about their world, and this leads to powerful and provocative discussions with teachers. As one teacher in an IGE session stated, 'We want our students to discover, to investigate, to inquire.'

INTERDISCIPLINARY LINKS

This unit is an interdisciplinary unit. Although it is presented here with an Australian Curriculum: Science content description as the starting point, it is not subject-specific, since the concepts driving the unit have relevance across all learning areas.

STEP 5: CONCEPTUAL UNDERSTANDING How can the understanding goals be written as a single statement?	The process of investigation leads to new discoveries.
STEP 4: CONCEPTS What concepts are the focus for the unit?	• investigation • process • discovery
STEP 3: UNDERSTANDING GOALS What 3–4 things should students understand by the end of the unit?	Students will understand … • the purpose of investigation • the processes involved in investigation • the connection between investigation and discovery
STEP 2: ASK Why is the unit compelling? Why is the unit significant? Why is the unit intriguing?	• The unit is compelling because investigation provides young children with opportunities to be curious, inquire and discover new ideas. • The unit is significant because through the process of investigation we are able to discover more about our world and who we are. • The unit is intriguing because young children naturally investigate and should be provided with provocations that promote investigation.

STEP 1: CONTENT
 	
What is the content to be explored in the unit?
	Australian Curriculum: Science
	Foundation Year
	• Science involves observing, asking questions about, and describing changes in, objects and events (ACSHE013)
	  • recognising that observation is an important part of exploring and investigating the things and places around us
	  • sharing observations with others and communicating their experiences
	  • exploring and observing using the senses: hearing, smell, touch, sight and taste

Table 2.6   Case study 3: Interdisciplinary unit for Foundation Year

CASE STUDY 4
HISTORY UNIT
YEAR 4

SETTING THE SCENE

Often in the humanities and social sciences, learning is determined by the need to provide sufficient coverage of a wide-ranging and content-heavy curriculum. History teachers who use the IGE model often find that by teaching through concepts instead of content, they can provide a lens for students to make sense of unfamiliar historical events and explorations without having to include endless facts and figures. Rather than teaching content for its own sake, teachers begin to see that they can use case studies of historical events and figures – for example, the travels of Captain Cook or the voyage of the First Fleet – to highlight deeper concepts that underpin the learning.

When a history unit likes this is implemented in classrooms, the broader focus on exploration as a concept creates some great discussion. Teachers comment that their students are making connections to Australia as it is today, to their own family histories and to other historical explorations without needing explicit introduction to this content. Because the concepts identified are compelling, significant and intriguing for the students, they function effectively to support more in-depth and transferable understanding.

INTERDISCIPLINARY LINKS

This unit provides a great opportunity for students to think about the historical events and discoveries that have created change and shaped societies from a range of different angles. Relevant content descriptions could include the following:

↘ Australian Curriculum: Health and Physical Education for Years 3 and 4

- Research own heritage and cultural identities, and explore strategies to respect and value diversity (ACPPS042)

↘ Australian Curriculum: German for Years 3 and 4

- Describe their own experiences of learning and using German and explore their sense of identity, including elements such as family, cultural heritage and friends (ACLGEC130)

STEP 5: CONCEPTUAL UNDERSTANDING How can the understanding goals be written as a single statement?	Motivation to explore leads to new discoveries that can shape and change society.
STEP 4: CONCEPTS What concepts are the focus for the unit?	• exploration • motivation • discovery • change
STEP 3: UNDERSTANDING GOALS What 3–4 things should students understand by the end of the unit?	Students will understand … • the factors that motivate exploration • that exploration brings about change for people, places and society • that exploration leads to new understandings about the past, present and future • how we can explore to discover
STEP 2: ASK Why is the unit compelling? Why is the unit significant? Why is the unit intriguing?	• The unit is compelling because it enlightens students about their own place and time, revealing how the past has shaped what their world is like now. • The unit is significant because exploration plays a pivotal role in shaping the present and future. • The unit is intriguing because it can be explored through evidence of the past, such as photographs and artefacts.

STEP 1: CONTENT
 	
What is the content to be explored in the unit?
	Australian Curriculum: Humanities and Social Sciences
	Year 4
	• The journey(s) of AT LEAST ONE world navigator, explorer or trader up to the late eighteenth century, including their contacts with other societies and any impacts (ACHASSK084)
	  • identifying key individuals and groups who established contacts with Africa, the Americas, Asia and Oceania during the European age of discovery
	  • investigating what motivated countries to explore and colonise
	  • examining the journey of one or more explorers (for example, Christopher Columbus, Vasco da Gama, Ferdinand Magellan), using navigation maps to reconstruct their journeys
	  • examining the impact of European exploration or colonisation on ONE society
	  • investigating networks of exchange and what was exchanged between different groups of people (for example, ideas, spices, food, slaves)
	  • recognising that people from many continents have explored parts of the world (for example, Zheng He, Ibn Battuta)

Table 2.7   Case study 4: History unit for Year 4

CASE STUDY 5
MUSIC UNIT
YEARS 5 AND 6

SETTING THE SCENE

For many single-subject or specialist teachers, the IGE model represents a new approach to curriculum planning. In our work with teachers of music, the conversations have shifted to focus on understanding rather than just skills. The discussion involves the consideration of which concepts can be included in the unit.

The clarification of a conceptual focus gives depth to the musical experience as well as providing opportunities for student reflection on the concepts, resulting in students' ongoing adjustment of their compositions. Music teachers who embed skill development within a conceptual framework provide a scaffold for understanding how the selected concepts connect to performance and production.

INTERDISCIPLINARY LINKS

The concepts of communication, performance and audience are especially important in creative fields such as English, foreign languages and arts subjects. The following content descriptions could be used to give an interdisciplinary dimension to the teaching of these concepts:

↘ Australian Curriculum: English for Year 5

- Use interaction skills, for example paraphrasing, questioning and interpreting non-verbal cues and choose vocabulary and vocal effects appropriate for different audiences and purposes (ACELY1796)

↘ Australian Curriculum: French for Years 5 and 6

- Interact using descriptive and expressive language to share ideas, relate experiences and express feelings such as concern or sympathy (ACLFRC037)

↘ Australian Curriculum: Dance for Years 5 and 6

- Perform dance using expressive skills to communicate a choreographer's ideas, including performing dances of cultural groups in the community (ACADAM011)

STEP 5: CONCEPTUAL UNDERSTANDING How can the understanding goals be written as a single statement?	Performance involves applying musical concepts to create compositions that are interpreted by an audience.
STEP 4: CONCEPTS What concepts are the focus for the unit?	• communication • composition • performance • audience
STEP 3: UNDERSTANDING GOALS What 3–4 things should students understand by the end of the unit?	Students will understand … • how to use musical concepts to arrange compositions • how performance is informed by a knowledge of musical elements and techniques • the role of the audience when creating music
STEP 2: ASK Why is the unit compelling? Why is the unit significant? Why is the unit intriguing?	• The unit is compelling as the requirement of performance asks students to think about how to communicate with their listeners. • The unit is significant due to the fact that students are encouraged to continually reflect and refine in order to better communicate their ideas. As with any aspect of learning, reflection leads to improvement. • The unit is intriguing as students must ensure that what they want to present comes through in their composition.

STEP 1: CONTENT
 	
What is the content to be explored in the unit?
	Australian Curriculum: Music
	Years 5 and 6
	• Rehearse and perform music including music they have composed by improvising, sourcing and arranging ideas and making decisions to engage an audience (ACAMUM090)
	  • improvising and experimenting with combinations of sounds and technologies to create moods and atmospheres
	  • organising, developing and refining ideas by experimenting with structure
	  • exploring rhythm, pitch and dynamics and expression to create contrast, repetition and balance to develop compositions for performance
	  • Considering viewpoints – forms and elements: For example – Which style of music is this? What musical clues helped you to decide?
	  • presenting performances using internet-based technologies, including social media

Table 2.8   Case study 5: Music unit for Years 5 and 6

TEACHER FEEDBACK ON THE IGE MODEL FOR FORMULATING CONCEPTUAL UNDERSTANDINGS

We have had many positive accounts from teachers about the model. It is clear that it has assisted them greatly in their development of conceptual understandings. For those working in teams, it has provided a collective understanding of the unit. Below are some reflective comments from teachers who have used the model for developing conceptual understandings.

- *This model makes so much sense! We have been trying to develop the conceptual understanding first. That explains why we have been spending so long trying to develop it. We've been making it up from thin air without any knowledge of what the purpose of the unit is conceptually. This model is much better, as we build up to the conceptual understanding.*

- *The IGE model could be used as a tool to identify the balance of conceptual coverage, both within year-level teams and also across the school from Years F–10. We can also see that the model could inform starting points for identifying interdisciplinary or transdisciplinary links.*

- *We were able to use the model to work through the process of constructing a concept-based unit with more clarity, taking the time needed and giving due consideration to every step of the process. It was slow; we didn't even finish developing our key questions; but everything we did was a) rock solid and b) agreed upon by everyone present.*

- *Defining what we want students to understand has given considerable clarity to the development of units in terms of conceptual understanding. We can see the conceptual links within the subject but also opportunity for interdisciplinary connections.*

CHAPTER 3: CONCEPTUAL LEARNING AND INQUIRY

WHAT IS CONCEPTUAL INQUIRY?

In past IGE workshop sessions, some teachers have expressed their worry that since our process entails the development of rigorous goals for conceptual understanding, the space for autonomous student inquiry might be limited. Does the IGE Model for Conceptual Understanding allow room for inquiry beyond the scope of the understanding goals? In fact, IGE is committed to ensuring that learning remains driven by student curiosity and wonder, and we firmly believe that a conceptual approach to learning is the best way to ensure that inquiry remains paramount.

Conceptual learning provides an ideal structure for authentic inquiry. According to McCoy & Ketterlin-Geller (2004), it is 'because most students cannot link facts to concepts' that 'classroom teachers must take responsibility for identifying concepts within the curriculum, an explicit and overt act' (p. 89). By contrast, the higher-level thinking skill of applying acquired knowledge to real-world situations is much more accessible if the conceptual context has already been defined.

When concepts are emphasised over content, there is no limit to the range of topics that students may investigate through a conceptual lens. But it is crucial that teachers allow time for students to pursue their own inquiries as an extension of the guided teacher inquiry, as this shows respect for students' growing independence as learners and provides motivation for further discoveries. For inquiry to be successful, students must be able to personally connect to the concepts, so their existing knowledge and understandings should be valued as stepping-stones to further mastery. Blythe & Associates (1998) suggest that as teaching of the unit progresses, additional understanding goals can be added that are derived from students' interest and inquiries. Table 3.1 (p. 34) explains more about the roles that students and teachers play during the conceptual inquiry process.

When IGE works with teachers to improve a unit by shifting the focus from content to concepts, it opens up the opportunity for student-led inquiry. One seminar participant, who was trying to create a unit on digital citizenship, started out by saying, 'I'm really finding it hard to teach this through inquiry'. The problem was that she was not teaching using concepts and was finding the prescribed content too restrictive. Upon further questioning, we suggested that she might instead teach the topic through the concepts of identity and expression. As soon we mentioned this, she said, 'I can see it already! I can think of ideas around this that are really inquiry-based'.

TEACHER'S ROLE	STUDENT'S ROLE
Show curiosity and a desire to learn	
Teachers approach conceptual inquiry with enthusiasm and excitement. Because they appreciate that conceptual inquiry can move in unexpected directions, they believe it is okay to reply, 'I don't know, I wonder – let's find out'. They model and ask open-ended questions that encourage investigation and experimentation.	Students show curiosity about the concepts being taught and take an active part in the inquiry. They recognise that in learning through concepts instead of content, they have access to endless possibilities and are able to follow new, previously unimagined directions for inquiry throughout the learning process.
Co-construct meaning	
Teachers model the conceptual inquiry process in their instruction, making the process of inquiry visible in the classroom. They facilitate, listen, discuss, clarify, support and monitor to help students develop their skills and thought processes. Strategic facilitation is provided throughout the unit to guide students in taking more and more responsibility in investigations.	Students work cooperatively with both the teacher and their peers to continually build on their understanding of the concepts in focus. When learning in collaborative situations, students co-construct conceptual understanding, in that they constantly re-evaluate and build new construct through the sharing different perspectives.
Ask meaningful questions	
Teachers plan conceptual questions that will drive the unit and engage students in wonder. Throughout the unit, they keep a list of the questions, issues and problems that arise during discussion as prompts for further investigation. They may also seek to encourage student wonderings by teaching their learners about what effective questioning looks like.	Students are empowered to ask relevant questions that connect to prior knowledge and enhance learning. Young children may not have the language required to pose meaningful questions; but it is important to remember that this is not a prerequisite for inquiry. We suggest that teachers observe children and listen to them carefully to see where their interests lie.
Define and solve problems	
Teachers provide openings for students to brainstorm possible challenges that may arise and discuss potential solutions. They continually build student capacity for planning and problem-solving.	Within a conceptual approach to learning, students are not just problem-solvers; they are also problem-definers. Students define problems that are connected to the concepts and consider how they can solve those problems.
Reflect	
Teachers coordinate support systems and reflective strategies that help students move through the inquiry process. They become aware of teachable moments resulting from conceptual misconceptions and challenge learners to move forward in developing skills of inquiry.	Students continually reflect on their understanding of the concepts, understanding goals and conceptual understanding. This reflection enables them to consider their previous ideas and evaluate how these have changed. It also gives students the opportunity to re-examine original thoughts, make adjustments and set new goals for their learning.

Table 3.1   Teacher and student roles in the conceptual inquiry process

PROCESSES FOR CONCEPTUAL INQUIRY

It is important to note that inquiry is not a linear step-by-step process, but rather a cluster of overlapping processes that can be utilised, combined and revisited as the inquiry takes shape. In our workshop sessions with educators, IGE outline seven major processes that make up the inquiry framework: connection, provocation, critical wondering, investigation, reflection, representation and transformation (see Figure 4.1). Teachers should aim to incorporate most if not all of these elements in order to facilitate successful inquiry, but students' knowledge, experiences and interests should guide when and how they manifest. Inquiry demands critical participation by the learner and time for reflection to make adjustments and decisions about the learning. It can be collaborative or individual.

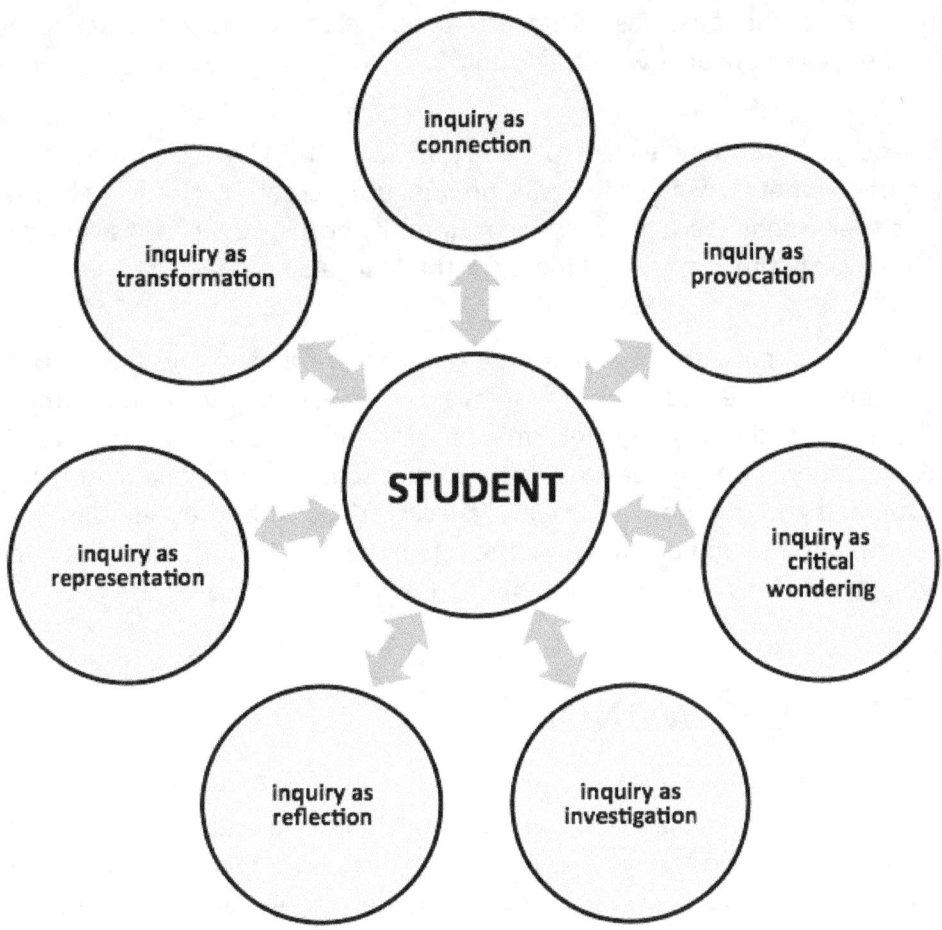

Figure 3.1   The processes of conceptual inquiry

INQUIRY AS CONNECTION

Inquiry provides a way for students to make meaning from their learning by exploring their own connections to it. In a conceptual unit, the process of inquiry as connection means that concepts are explored in ways that are relevant to students' prior knowledge and experience. These real-world connections are revisited and strengthened throughout the unit to help students build towards conceptual understanding.

Inquiry as connection may occur spontaneously, but teachers should also work to motivate the process. For example, in a unit with the conceptual understanding, 'People's beliefs and values form their identity and influence their actions', one way to connect the concept of identity to students' own lives would be to have each student bring in an object from home to add to an anonymous display. The class could then discuss which student they think owns which object, and why.

INQUIRY AS PROVOCATION

The aim of inquiry as provocation is to engage students in the learning and make them curious about the unit. The selection of resources is critical here, as provocations must be stimulating and age-appropriate to ensure student engagement. Objects and activities that can be used as provocations include classroom design, excursions, class visits, artefacts, literature and any other resources that will motivate students to explore concepts within the unit.

Inquiry as provocation is closely related to inquiry as connection. While connection piques student interest by drawing upon what they already know, provocations create excitement by making students curious about what they might learn. In a conceptual unit, both provocations and connections are invoked specifically to clarify the conceptual focus for the learners.

Provocations should align with the concepts that are the focus of the unit in order to provoke student excitement about where the learning might go. For instance, in a unit with the conceptual understanding, 'The needs of living things determine their habitats', teachers could tap into inquiry as provocation by taking students on a guided walk around the school grounds, encouraging them to take note of the plants, animals and other environmental characteristics that they see. Discuss with students how these features came to be, and explain how the school garden is itself a habitat. Once it has been introduced through provocations, the definition of habitat is built upon over the course of the unit.

INQUIRY AS CRITICAL WONDERING

Teachers must provide a learning environment that promotes student questions, utterances and wonderment about their learning. Critical wondering should be encouraged throughout the unit. Finding ways to collect student wonderings is essential to informing student-initiated inquiries; teachers might try setting up a critical wondering wall, handing out individual journals or making notes.

When learning is conceptual, critical wonderings are built from ongoing provocation related to the concepts. Moving from factual questions to questions of more complexity is key in guiding students to identify the independent inquiries they choose to pursue. In a unit guided by the conceptual understanding that 'Water is a limited resource that is fundamental for life', teachers might provide students with actual data on water use then elicit their questioning and wonderings about this information. The data could then provide the basis for investigation into the environmental impact of water use, provoking further inquiry into the concepts of conservation and sustainability.

The most important aspect of critical wondering is that the student wonderings collected are incorporated into the unit. This can be done several ways. One option is to have the teacher or students choose learning engagements that lead to investigate the questions. Another is that the teacher prompts students to go about finding their own answers to the questions. Finally, inquiry groups or individual inquiries may be developed around questions that students pose. Questions are collected and collated and students decide which question they wish to explore.

INQUIRY AS INVESTIGATION

During the process of inquiry as investigation, students actively set out to discover new information about their conceptual questions and critical wonderings. Knowledge, skills and concepts intertwine throughout this process, as students make discoveries that bring the conceptual understanding of the unit into focus. Teachers should ensure that any sustained investigations are planned in advance and that the resources necessary for the investigation are accessible.

Investigations can be teacher facilitated or learner driven, and they may be carried out in groups or by individuals. One effective way to prompt investigation is to create a wall chart of student critical wonderings or a list of big questions that arise during discussion and ask students to choose the one question that is most significant for them – the question they really want to know more about.

INQUIRY AS REFLECTION

The reflection process informs the inquiry, guides goal-setting and suggests new directions. It is also key to ensuring that teachers identify and address differentiated needs among their students. As Marian Small (2013) states, 'follow-up discussions play a significant role in cementing learning and building confidence in students. Thus, it is important for teachers to employ strategies that will optimize the effectiveness of follow-up discussions to benefit students at all developmental levels' (p. 10).

Reflection differs from critical wondering in that critical wondering is about what students will learn, whereas reflection looks back on what students have learnt. Teachers should plan to ensure that there will be opportunities for students to reflect on their understanding throughout the unit. Through the process of reflection, students should aim to rethink, demonstrate and celebrate their new learning.

There are many effective teaching strategies that can help to stimulate reflection, including circle time, think-pair-share, student journals and more. Teachers may like to guide the process by asking using a specific prompt and setting a time limit for reflection. In a unit on the concept of friendship, for instance, students might be given one minute to reflect upon the prompt, 'Describe what is most important for you about friendship'.

INQUIRY AS REPRESENTATION

Students represent their inquiry when they share their new knowledge with others. The process of representation asks students to identify what in their learning is important to know and then decide how best to communicate it. After students share their learning, they should be given time to reflect on new learnings and make connections with prior understandings. From here, new critical wonderings and fresh opportunities for investigation will arise.

To avoid confusion, teachers may want to set a specific task to guide the process of representation. For instance, in a unit with the conceptual understanding, 'Technologies increasingly enrich and impact on the global lives of people, culture and society', students could be asked to decide on a technology and give a presentation predicting how the design may change and what the impact of that change will be on the environment.

When students are allowed to choose their own presentation formats, we have found it useful early on in the unit to brainstorm all the possible ways in which they might represent their inquiry – such as essays, slide shows, videos, craft projects, role plays and so on. Otherwise, some groups will spend so much time debating about the mode of presentation that they lose focus on the inquiry itself. Once the list of possibilities is visible, students focus on the concepts rather than the format and often modify their thinking about how to best represent their new understandings. It is also useful to have students justify why they have chosen a particular type of presentation, as this can help to clarify the suitability of the format.

INQUIRY AS TRANSFORMATION

Inquiry as transformation occurs when students begin to build upon the concepts they have studied by applying them autonomously in real-world contexts. This might happen during the course of the unit, but it is equally common at a later stage when students are seen to make connections to prior understandings. Whether in the form of changed behaviours, altered attitudes or the transference of new theories and ideas, authentic application of concepts is the key indicator that student thinking has transformed as a result of conceptual learning. Table 3.2 lays out some questions that teachers might use to reflect on and devise learning engagements for each process.

TIPS FOR CONCEPTUAL INQUIRY

Inasmuch as conceptual learning provides an ideal framework for inquiry, the inquiry process also enables conceptual thinking to evolve through the active co-construction of ideas between teacher and students. To facilitate this process, IGE has compiled the following list of tips and strategies to connect and expand conceptual understanding through inquiry.

- ⬎ **Ensure the focus remains on concepts.** In a conceptual unit, the content taught is used to underpin the conceptual ideas and is not the focus of the learning. One way to achieve this is to set up your classroom with explicit reminders of the concepts being studied. For instance, you might display significant objects or artefacts next to critical questions designed to engage student interest in key concepts. Or, tools like noticeboards, graffiti boards or word walls can be used for documenting the conceptual questions and critical wonderings of students.

- ⬎ **Present intriguing provocations to engage student interest.** To ensure that students are actively involved in processing their learning, create a range of learning engagements that centre on providing connections to the concepts. Photographs, videos, books, websites, artefacts and fieldwork can all stimulate conceptual inquiry. Spend time locating authentic

PROCESS	GUIDING QUESTIONS
Inquiry as connection	• What is compelling and significant in the world of my students? • How can I help students to uncover personal connections between their own lives and the concepts driving their learning? • What resources will encourage students to connect to the concepts?
Inquiry as provocation	• How will the provocations I have designed engage students in the concepts? • How will the provocations help me to ascertain student's prior knowledge? • What resources should I use to provoke student curiosity?
Inquiry as critical wondering	• What do students most want to know? What are the key questions arising from their wonderings? • What do students' wonderings reveal about their grasp of the conceptual understanding of the unit? • How will student's critical wonderings be collected or recorded? • How will students' critical wonderings be embedded in the inquiry?
Inquiry as investigation	• Have I identified a critical conceptual question or wondering? • Do I have a plan to guide the process of conceptual investigation? • What learning engagements will enable my students to work towards conceptual understanding? • Do these learning engagements utilise a range of real-world resources?
Inquiry as reflection	• What is the most significant idea that students have connected to? What prompted them to make this connection? • What is it students still want to understand or know? • At what level is students' current understanding of the concepts, understanding goal and conceptual understanding?
Inquiry as representation	• What are some of the mediums in which students could represent their learning? • Do students have the skills and understanding necessary to communicate their new knowledge to peers? • How will others be able to access the students' ideas or new findings?
Inquiry as transformation	• What are the big ideas students have gained from the inquiry? • What unexpected connections have students made during the inquiry process? • How has what students have learnt made a difference in their lives? • How can students use their new understanding to make a better world?

Table 3.2   Guiding inquiry questions for teachers

resources – both those that give access to the concepts and those that diversify interpretation of the concepts. Think carefully when selecting resources about how each item will engage students and stimulate their curiosity about the world.

↘ **Ask open-ended conceptual questions.** A powerful strategy to engage students and drive inquiry is to use well-designed conceptual questions. Conceptual questions invite authentic wondering, reflection and collaborative discourse, helping students to identify thinking processes, see the connections between ideas and build new understanding. Table 3.3 below outlines some of the main characteristics of and key criteria for effective conceptual questions.

CHARACTERISTICS OF CONCEPTUAL QUESTIONS	KEY CRITERIA FOR CONCEPTUAL QUESTIONS
• Conceptual questions suggest inquiry and invite investigation. • Conceptual questions are organisers and set the focus for the unit. • Conceptual questions are initiators of creative and critical thinking. • Conceptual questions are conceptual commitments focusing on key concepts implicit in the curriculum.	• Each student should be able to understand the key conceptual questions. • The language of the questions should be in broad terms that reflect the concepts. • There should be a logical sequence to and interconnection between a set of key conceptual questions. • Key conceptual questions can be visible in the classroom.

Table 3.3   Characteristics of and criteria for effective conceptual inquiry questions
Adapted from Greenville County Schools (n.d.)

Teachers often ask how they can get students to generate their own conceptual questions at the start of a unit. We find that students often ask the most authentic questions after they have had a chance to connect with the concepts. The teacher's questions and provocations are what initially drive investigation, and it is as a result of this process that we see students' own critical wonderings emerge. By listening attentively to students' thoughts while keeping the big ideas in mind, teachers are able to identify and develop important ideas in the discourse.

To assist teachers in devising questions for their inquiries, IGE has developed some examples of conceptual questions in a range of Australian Curriculum learning areas (see Table 3.4 opposite). For more great examples of conceptual questions, we recommend Heick's (2014) aptly named 'Giant list of really good essential questions'.

↘ **Connect concepts across the curriculum.** Where there is opportunity for authentic links across the curriculum, make time to consider how these connections might evolve through the classroom practice. For example, a teacher may choose to explore the concept of systems through the learning area of science, but there are also many authentic connections to systems as a concept in maths, languages, humanities and social sciences, the arts and physical education. For teachers, a knowledge of the vertical curriculum is critical when it comes to identifying opportunities to make these connections.

LEARNING AREA	CONCEPTUAL QUESTIONS
Science	• If we alter some of the variables in this experiment, how do you think the outcome will change? • In what ways do people use science within their everyday lives? • Why is the data structured in that way?
Mathematics	• What is pattern? • How are these operations related to one another? • In what ways might you explain, demonstrate or draw this process?
Humanities and social sciences	• How do historical events shape the present day? • Why is it important to care for the places in our community? • How do we know whether a piece of evidence is reliable?
English	• Why is literacy important in our society? • Do stories need a beginning, middle and end? Why or why not? • In what ways does culture influence the language we use?
Technologies	• How does this design solution meet community needs? • What are some positive and negative ways in which digital technologies have changed our society? • Why do some types of visuals represent information better than others?
Health and physical education	• How are people altered through their relationships with others? • In what ways does the media shape our view of the world and ourselves? • Why is it important to promote fair play during team sports?
The arts	• Should art be political? Why or why not? • How do different types of art inform one another? • What role does art play in the evolution of society and culture?
Languages	• How does learning about another culture help us to better understand our own? • Is it good for a society to include people from diverse language backgrounds? • What are the benefits of learning an additional language?

Table 3.4   Conceptual inquiry questions for students

In addition, students themselves may spot opportunities for conceptual connections. One teacher in an IGE workshop session shared that when her class explored the concept of adaptability through volleyball in terms of movement and design, the students pointed out the relevance of this concept for their science unit about climate and environment.

↘ **Vary your level of involvement.** Teachers must be responsive to the needs of students at each phase of the inquiry. In the 'inquiry as connection' and 'inquiry as provocation' processes, the teacher will be very active: organising resources, designing learning experiences and establishing the current knowledge level of the students. In the 'inquiry as representation' or 'inquiry as reflection' processes, it is the student who drives the learning, devising ways of making their learning visible to others and reflecting on what they now know and understand.

↘ **Continually find ways to stimulate reflection about concepts**. Provide students with oral or written tools for reflection such as sentence starters, learning logs, exit cards and other graphic organisers. Strategically plan activities that will allow students to reflect on their conceptual learning, as it is this co-construction of knowledge that will provide students with opportunity to make sense and articulate their understanding of the concepts being explored.

↘ **Encourage students to collaborate and discuss their ideas with each other.** By sharing ideas and listening to other perspectives, students critically engage with their own and others' interpretation of the concepts. Pair or group activities that have been carefully designed to engage students in collaborative thinking can provide new avenues for investigation.

↘ **Make sure that all presentations relate to key concepts**. Build in opportunities for ongoing reflection while students are preparing to represent the results of their inquiries. Encourage students to ask the following questions:

- Am I satisfied with my representation of these ideas?

- How well does my representation address the concepts we have been exploring?

- What else might I add to or leave out of my representation?

↘ **Monitor student inquiries beyond the classroom.** When students begin to identify real-world applications of the concepts they are studying in school, we consider this an indication of significant progress towards conceptual understanding. To monitor this process, create regular opportunities in class for students to share ideas for and experiences of continuing conceptual inquiry – such as a household renovation project where the student can see the concepts of design and technology in real terms. If possible, teachers could even solicit observations from parents about how students have been using concepts in their everyday lives.

↘ **Rigorously evaluate the effectiveness of the inquiry and address areas in need of improvement.** To help teachers do this, we have produced a comprehensive checklist for effective conceptual inquiry (Table 3.5, pp. 43–45). We recommend that teachers use this checklist at regular intervals throughout the unit in order to remain engaged in the progress of the learning. The checklist is available for download at **go.hbe.com.au**.

ROLE OF TEACHER	SELDOM		SOMETIMES		OFTEN
	1	2	3	4	5
Teacher facilitates the co-construction of meaning through conceptual questioning.					
Teacher designs open-ended conceptual questions to promote thinking.					
Teacher engages students in conceptual provocations to clarify and make personal connection to concepts.					
Teacher ensures the focus in the classroom is towards the conceptual understandings and concepts and not always the content or correct answer.					
Teacher uses the language of the concepts authentically and as often as possible to assist students in making connections and seeing relationships.					
Teacher provides opportunities for students to connect the understanding and concepts beyond the classroom, particularly to the real world.					
Teacher collects statements students make about the concept.					
Teacher ensures all presentations connect back to the concept (big idea).					
Teacher connects concepts across the curriculum.					
Teacher offers opportunities for students to share their assumptions and to reflect on their thinking of a concept.					
Teacher encourages students to take risks in their conceptual thinking and to consider other points of view and evidence.					
Comments					

Table 3.5   Checklist for effective conceptual inquiry (1 of 3)

ROLE OF STUDENT	SELDOM		SOMETIMES		OFTEN
	1	2	3	4	5
Students are active participants in their own conceptual learning, creating new ideas and expanding their thinking.					
Students relate new conceptual learning to the real world beyond the classroom.					
Students construct meaning for the concepts through collaboration and discussion.					
Students continually find ways to reflect on the concept.					
Students consider other points of view and evidence.					
Comments					

LEARNING ENVIRONMENT	SELDOM		SOMETIMES		OFTEN
	1	2	3	4	5
Conceptual thinking is made visible through the display of graphic organisers, thinking tools and so on.					
Classroom design allows for the regrouping and grouping of students to engage in conceptual ideas.					
Learning areas encourage student-initiated inquiries.					
A variety of materials and resources connected to the concepts being studied are available.					
The concept is displayed so that students can add their understanding to it using sticky notes or other strategies.					
Displays and artefacts reflect the concepts being studied.					
Comments					

Table 3.5   Checklist for effective conceptual inquiry (2 of 3)

ASSESSMENT STRATEGIES	SELDOM		SOMETIMES		OFTEN
	1	2	3	4	5
Assessment tasks are designed to assess understanding goals and conceptual understandings.					
Assessment tasks are explicitly connected to the concepts.					
A variety of rich conceptual learning engagements are used to meet the diversity of learning.					
Students are organised in a range of groupings to provide for collaborative thinking around conceptual ideas.					
Student critical wonderings for student-initiated inquiry are derived from the conceptual ideas.					
Comments					

Table 3.5   Checklist for effective conceptual inquiry (3 of 3)

CHAPTER 4:
CONCEPTUAL LEARNING AND
ASSESSMENT

It is important within any planning process that educators are explicitly aware of what they are looking for with regard to understanding. When assessing conceptual learning, there are two primary aspects to consider:

1. The student's grasp of the understanding goals of the unit.

2. The student's comprehension of the concepts driving the unit.

ASSESSING UNDERSTANDING GOALS

IGE's approach to assessing understanding goals is to use a four-level learning continuum. By creating a learning continuum for each understanding goal, educators have an explicit and consistent way to assess each student's ongoing development towards mastery of that goal. Students will have varying levels of understanding in relation to each goal, so educators should identify and use an assessment strategy that provides clear criteria for monitoring student progress. Prior to and throughout the unit, teachers should administer regular formative assessments using the levels of understanding in order to inform further learning engagements. The levels of understanding are also used to develop possible summative tasks for the unit.

Table 4.1 (p. 48) outlines the four levels of IGE's learning continuum, which is inspired by Webb's (2002) Depth-of-Knowledge Levels. It includes key verbs associated with each level that can assist teachers in thinking about how to formulate their own continuums. Also included in the table are suggestions for learning engagements designed to provide teachers with strategies for gathering evidence of understanding.

When developing levels for each understanding goal, teachers should ask themselves the following question: 'What would mastery look like in relation to this understanding goal?' Due to how conceptually integrated they are, teachers may find it logical to combine more than one understanding goal in a single continuum.

LEVEL OF UNDERSTANDING	RELATED VERBS	LEARNING ENGAGEMENTS
Level 1: Recalling Students recall knowledge that relates to the understanding goal.	• remember • state • name • retell • identify • recognise • label	• make a list • create an illustration • label items • answer quiz questions • recite from memory
Level 2: Describing Going beyond recall to describe involves students describing in some detail information related to the understanding goal. Students begin to make inferences and interpret their understandings.	• categorise • describe • interpret • classify • define • determine	• create a cause-and-effect graphic organiser • group similar items • construct a model • write a description
Level 3: Explaining and connecting Students make comparisons between existing knowledge and the concepts. They are able to explain in detail what they have learnt and the connections within it.	• compare • contrast • connect • explain • distinguish • formulate • differentiate	• create a concept map (p. 52) • make a Venn diagram • distinguish between items • explain connections between ideas • compare and contrast ideas with those of peers
Level 4: Analysing and applying Analysing and evaluating through reasoning and application, involves students analysing in detail how everything is connected. Students can make new connections and analyse with reasoning and logical evidence the reasons these connections exist.	• evaluate • analyse • reason • synthesise • critique • interpret • prove • transfer • apply	• create a concept map (p. 52), accompanied by a detailed explanation of the reasoning behind it • construct a model, then analyse it and make improvements • debate ideas with peers • write a persuasive text • problem-solve and problem-pose

Table 4.1   Levels of understanding
Adapted from Webb (2002)

ASSESSING UNDERSTANDING GOALS FORMATIVELY

To assess student learning formatively, educators develop 'learning engagements', also referred to as 'performances of understanding':

> *Performances of understanding help students build and demonstrate their understanding. Although a 'performance' might sound like a final event, performances of understanding are principally learning activities. They give both you and your students a chance to see their understanding develop in new and challenging situations over time. (Blythe & Associates 1998, pp. 62–63)*

Once the understanding goal and levels of understanding have been established, teachers can brainstorm learning engagements that will help them to monitor a student's level of understanding. Table 4.1 contains a list of suggested learning engagements for each level that can be undertaken individually, as a group or even as a peer assessment task. The evidence gained from the learning engagements provides specific and helpful feedback for students and teachers in order to assist them in building the levels of understanding.

As an example, consider a Year 5 unit on digital citizenship with the following understanding goals:

- ↘ Identify different types of digital media.
- ↘ Describe the ways we use digital media as a tool for expression.

These understanding goals have been combined in a single continuum because in order to understand the ways digital media is used as a tool for expression, the students first had to explore all the different types of digital media. Table 4.2 (p. 50) represents the learning continuum a teacher might devise for these understanding goals.

ASSESSING UNDERSTANDING GOALS SUMMATIVELY

A summative assessment task should clearly demonstrate evidence of each student's understanding. In order to ensure that the summative task is closely connected to the understanding goals, it may be worth brainstorming a few summative assessment tasks at that can be reviewed as the unit progresses. It is important to note that you do not necessarily need a summative assessment for each understanding goal, as a single summative assessment may include two or more understanding goals.

Many teachers design summative assessment tasks that assess skills or knowledge rather than understanding. During IGE's work with educators, teachers have repeatedly stated that using the levels of understanding significantly helped to clarify what they were looking for with regard to student mastery. For example, a music teacher commented, 'I can already see where some of my students are along the levels, which is great as I now know where to go next'.

UNDERSTANDING GOALS	• Different types of digital media • Ways we use digital media as a tool for expression
Level 1: Recall	Students can state the different types of digital media and their purpose.
Level 2: Going beyond recall to describe	Students will describe the different types of digital media available and define how each digital media tool can be used. They will infer what people want to share on digital media and why they choose that media tool.
Level 3: Describing and explaining comparisons and connections	Students will connect the different types of digital media available and explain how each digital media tool can be used. They will make the connection between what people want to share and why they chose that media tool. They will distinguish between the different media in terms of how much expression each form enables.
Level 4: Analysing and evaluating through reasoning	Students will analyse the different types of digital media available and evaluate how each digital media tool can be used. They will critique each tool, stating why people chose that tool and if it was the best choice. They will evaluate the level of expression that each tool enables, using evidence to back up their findings. Students can apply this knowledge and understanding when expressing themselves.

Table 4.2   Levels of understanding

ASSESSING CONCEPTUAL LEARNING

The other aspect of assessing conceptual learning is to assess student's understanding of the concepts driving the unit. It is important that throughout the unit, students are building their understanding and knowledge of the concepts in ways that will be transferable in and outside the classroom. The following formative assessment tools can be employed before, during and at the conclusion of the unit to determine how students are progressing when it comes to understanding and making connections between concepts. Note that many of the strategies listed in the Appendix: Strategies for Conceptual Learning (pp. 81–86) can also be used as formative assessment.

⬎ **Index card summaries and questions.** Throughout the unit, distribute index cards and ask students to fill them in according to the following prompts:

- Side 1: List what you understand about the concept, then word your understandings as a summary statement.

- Side 2: Identify something about the concept that you do not yet fully understand and word it as a question.

↘ **Hand signals.** Ask students to display a designated hand signal to indicate their understanding of the concept:

- Thumbs up: I understand and can explain it.
- Thumbs down: I do not yet understand.
- Thumb midway: I'm not completely sure about it.

↘ **One-minute Q&A.** The teacher asks a question connected to the concept and students are given a minute to answer the questions. This allows teachers to determine students current understanding of the concept.

↘ **Agree or disagree.** Present students with common or predictable misconceptions and non-misconceptions about the concept. Ask them whether they agree or disagree with what is presented and have them explain why.

↘ **Student conference.** The teacher conducts a one-on-one conversation with each student, using carefully designed questions to check their level of understanding. This is particularly good for young children who may not have developed the necessary writing skills to transcribe their thoughts.

↘ **Stop and pause.** This activity provides a chance for students to stop and reflect on the concept that they have been learning about. The teacher pauses the class and has the students work in small groups to discuss their current understanding of the concept. Sentence starters to prompt discussion could include the following:

- I changed my ideas about …
- I now know …
- I was surprised about …
- I felt …
- I connected to …
- I still want to know …

↘ **Observation.** Walk around the classroom and observe students as they work to check for understanding and for misconceptions connected to the concepts. Record what it is you hear through anecdotal records or checklists.

↘ **Self-assessment.** Students collect information about their own learning, analyse what it reveals about their progress towards the concept and plan the next steps in their inquiry.

↘ **Concept brainstorm.** Ideas connected to the concepts – such as pictures, readings and objects – are placed around the room. Students look through the different ideas and work in groups to brainstorm conceptual connections. They discuss the ideas in groups and share their understanding with the class.

⬊ **Concept word splash.** The concept is written or drawn in the centre of a sheet of poster paper. The students record, write or sketch all the words and images that they can think of in relation to the concept. Students then look for connections, drawing lines to connect the different ideas when they see relationships to create clusters of ideas. These clusters are then discussed.

⬊ **Concept map.** Students create a concept map that shows the connections between ideas linked to the concepts. Words are used to describe the relationship between the ideas. Concept maps enable students to continuously add their ideas and build their understanding of the concepts. They can be used for formative and summative assessment.

⬊ **Bus stop.** Sheets of poster paper are posted around the room, each with a different concept on it. Students are divided into groups based on the number of charts, so there is a group of students at each sheet of paper. Students brainstorm and write all the ideas they have on the paper. When the teacher gives the instruction, each group moves clockwise to the next bus stop. They read what others have written, and if they agree they put a tick next to what has been written, then add their own ideas. They cannot write what has already been written. This cycle continues until the students get back to their original sheet.

CHAPTER 5: PLANNING CONCEPTUAL LEARNING

PRINCIPLES OF CONCEPTUAL PLANNING

Conceptual planning is a practical process, based on strong theoretical underpinnings about how students learn. Authentic conceptual planning is grounded in the following principles:

> ↘ **Planning is responsive to students needs.** Planning needs to be ongoing, dynamic and organic. The planning document should continue to evolve throughout the life of the unit, developing in response to student wonderings. It is an accurate record of the learning that took place throughout the unit.

> ↘ **Planning reflects the conceptual components.** Learning engagements and assessments are focused around conceptual understandings, concepts and understanding goals.

> ↘ **Planning includes identifying knowledge and skills to support learning.** Skills and knowledge that support conceptual understanding are usually identified from curriculum documents. The skills and knowledge are explicitly planned for and taught as part of the unit.

> ↘ **Planning is collaborative.** Planning meetings involve the whole team responsible for teaching the unit, including specialist teachers. This guarantees that the teaching and learning is consistent across subject areas.

> ↘ **Planning involves students in co-designing learning.** Students co-design or co-construct their inquiries throughout the unit. When planning units, consider how these inquiries might be negotiated with students and documented.

> ↘ **Planning indicates both formative and summative assessment strategies.** Planning involves documenting what evidence of understanding will look like. By checking in with students using formative assessments, teachers are able to guide the learning to ensure a level of success in the summative tasks.

> ↘ **Planning involves inquiry as connection and provocation.** The significance of these two phases in the inquiry process is key to developing student curiosity around the conceptual focus of the unit. Learning engagements connect students with the concepts and provoke student curiosity and wonderings so they can actively seek to understand and make meaning.

➘ **Planning involves a variety of learning engagements and resources.** Teachers plan to use a range of teaching strategies and resources to engage and motivate students, enabling them to co-construct learning in meaningful and varied ways. By utilising a variety of engagements and resources, teachers are able to better cater to the learning needs and styles of all students.

CHECKLIST: PRINCIPLES OF PLANNING	YES	NO
Planning is responsive to students needs.		
Planning is authentically documented.		
Planning reflects the conceptual components.		
Planning includes identifying knowledge and skills to support learning.		
Planning is collaborative.		
Planning involves students in co-designing learning.		
Planning involves inquiry as connection and provocation in order to provide conceptual contexts for students.		
Planning involves a variety of learning engagements and resources.		

Table 5.1   Checklist for effective conceptual inquiry (3 of 3)

THE IGE TEMPLATE FOR PLANNING CONCEPTUAL LEARNING

IGE advocates for a curriculum planning process that is dynamic, flexible, ongoing and reflective. The planning document should continue to evolve throughout the life of the unit, developing and changing in response to student experience. Instead of adhering to a rigid, prescriptive approach to instruction, educators who teach through concepts support students to reflect on their learning and encourage the identification of further areas for investigation. Conceptual learning opens doors, allowing students to access the limitless possibilities for learning in the world around them.

The IGE Template for Planning Conceptual Learning (Table 5.2, pp. 55–58) has been designed to facilitate a conceptual planning process that is clear and coherent yet responsive and evolving. It represents the culmination of the theory of conceptual learning outlined in this book. Each section of the template can be revisited, modified or added to as students engage with the concepts through increasingly independent inquiry. The blank planning template is available for download at **go.hbe.com.au**.

STAGE 1: DEVELOPING CONCEPTS	
Conceptual understanding	
Concepts	

Understanding goals	Essential questions

Knowledge	Skills

Resources and learning environment	

Table 5.2   IGE Template for Planning Conceptual Learning (1 of 4)

STAGE 2: DEVELOPING UNDERSTANDING GOALS				
Understanding goal	Level 1	Level 2	Level 3	Level 4
Summative assessment ideas				

Table 5.2   IGE Template for Planning Conceptual Learning (2 of 4)

STAGE 3: DEVELOPING LEARNING ENGAGEMENTS	
Step 1: Planning before the unit begins	
Inquiry as connection and provocation	
Inquiry as critical wondering	
Step 2: Planning as the unit progresses	
Inquiry as investigation, representation, reflection and transformation	

Table 5.2   IGE Template for Planning Conceptual Learning (3 of 4)

STAGE 4: EVIDENCE-BASED REFLECTION	
What was important about what we did?	
Did we meet our goals?	
What changes would we make to the unit?	

Table 5.2   IGE Template for Planning Conceptual Learning (4 of 4)

HOW TO USE THE IGE TEMPLATE FOR PLANNING CONCEPTUAL LEARNING

Table 5.3 (pp. 58–60) contains an explanation of how to use each section of the IGE Template for Planning Conceptual Understanding.

STAGE 1: DEVELOPING CONCEPTS	
Conceptual understanding **Concepts**	Teachers embarking on the planning phase should already have developed concepts and a conceptual understanding for the unit using the IGE Model for Formulating Conceptual Understandings. For more information on the model, see Chapter 2: Formulating Conceptual Understandings (pp. 17–32).
Understanding goals	**Essential questions**
Teachers should already have developed understanding goals for the unit using the IGE Model for Formulating Conceptual Understandings. For more information, see Chapter 2 (pp. 17–32).	These can be developed prior to the unit and added to as students and teachers co-construct learning. Essential questions are connected to the understanding goals.

Table 5.3   Explanation of the IGE Template for Planning Conceptual Learning (1 of 3)

Knowledge	Skills
Knowledge is what students should know, while skills are what they should be able to do. The knowledge and skills listed in these sections will usually be drawn from the following documents: • national and state curriculum documents (for example, the Australian Curriculum) • scope and sequence documents • school- or teacher-devised standards documents • additional knowledge and skills as appropriate to the unit	

Resources and learning environment	Teachers identify resources they will need to enhance the learning. This includes people, places, films, videos, artefacts and books. It is suggested that where possible, teachers use real people, places, experiences and objects to ensure authenticity of learning and provide students with opportunities to connect to the real world. Teachers should also consider how the design of the learning spaces in the classroom and beyond can be used to engage and motivate learners.

STAGE 2: DEVELOPING UNDERSTANDING GOALS

Understanding goal	Level 1	Level 2	Level 3	Level 4
Levels of understanding enable teachers to create formative and summative assessments that are directly related to the understanding goals of the unit. Go to Chapter 4: Conceptual Learning and Assessment (pp. 47–52) for more information about developing levels of understanding.				

Summative assessment ideas

The summative assessment task or tasks will provide clear evidence of student understanding. The task may change as the unit progresses; these are initial ideas. It is important to note that you do not necessarily need a summative assessment for each understanding goal, as teachers may develop summative assessments that include two or more goals.

STAGE 3: DEVELOPING LEARNING ENGAGEMENTS

Step 1: Planning before the unit begins

Inquiry as connection and provocation	Teacher develop engagements that provide students with contexts for making personal connections to the concepts driving the unit. The provocations need to align with the conceptual focus of the unit and provoke student curiosity. It is from the provocations that students will begin to wonder and question. To learn more about the processes of conceptual inquiry, see Chapter 3: Conceptual Learning and Inquiry (pp. 33–45).

Table 5.3   Explanation of the IGE Template for Planning Conceptual Learning (2 of 3)

Inquiry as critical wondering	Student questions and wonderings are documented in this section. These need to be authentic and related to the unit. The questions are incorporated into the ongoing planning of the unit. To learn more about the processes of conceptual inquiry, see Chapter 3: Conceptual Learning and Inquiry (pp. 33–45).
Step 2: Planning as the unit progresses	
Inquiry as investigation, representation, reflection and transformation	Using evidence of understanding from Stage 2 of the planning template along with students' critical wonderings, teachers determine the next stages of planning. The resulting learning engagements evolve and in response to students' understanding of the conceptual focus of the unit and their application of skills and knowledge. To learn more about the processes of conceptual inquiry, see Chapter 3: Conceptual Learning and Inquiry (pp. 33–45). Teachers can also reference the levels of understanding for the unit (see Chapter 4, pp. 47–52) to develop relevant learning engagements.

STAGE 4: EVIDENCE-BASED REFLECTION
This section is completed as an ongoing reflection of the unit. It is important that student voice is incorporated into this section. The reflection is used to assist with ongoing planning.

Table 5.3   Explanation of the IGE Template for Planning Conceptual Learning (3 of 3)

CASE STUDIES OF THE IGE TEMPLATE FOR PLANNING CONCEPTUAL LEARNING

CASE STUDY 1
HABITATS UNIT
YEAR 1

Habitats is a key topic for science in the lower primary years. In discussion with many teams about the planning for this unit, it became clear that real-life investigations were being compromised to focus more on research from non-fiction texts and videos. After lengthy discussion as to the value of teaching young children to observe and annotate their scientific observations, it became evident that the teachers needed to think differently in order to map a more investigative and authentic conceptual inquiry.

The unit in Table 5.4 below is a combination of ideas from a few different teams with whom IGE has worked. It demonstrates how to make the shift from habitats as a topic to a conceptual unit that involves in-depth firsthand inquiry. The unit includes several local field investigations in order to support the inquiry.

STAGE 1: DEVELOPING CONCEPTS	
Conceptual understanding	The habitats of living things meet their needs in different ways.
Concepts	• habitat • needs • function

Understanding goals	Essential questions
Students will understand … • the needs of living things • different habitats and their features • how living things interact with the environment	• What is a habitat? • How do habitats meet the needs of living things? • How do living things interact with each other and the environment?

Knowledge	Skills
Australian Curriculum: Science Year 1 • Living things have a variety of external features (ACSSU017) • Living things live in different places where their needs are met (ACSSU211) • Science involves observing, asking questions about, and describing changes in, objects and events (ACSHE021) • People use science in their daily lives, including when caring for their environment and living things (ACSHE022) Australian Curriculum: Humanities and Social Sciences Year 1 • The natural, managed and constructed features of places, their location, how they change and how they can be cared for (ACHASSK031)	Australian Curriculum: Science Year 1 • Pose and respond to questions, and make predictions about familiar objects and events (ACSIS024) • Participate in guided investigations to explore and answer questions (ACSIS025) • Use informal measurements to collect and record observations, using digital technologies as appropriate (ACSIS026) • Use a range of methods to sort information, including drawings and provided tables through discussion, compare observations with predictions (ACSIS027) • Compare observations with those of others (ACSIS213) • Represent and communicate observations and ideas in a variety of ways (ACSIS029)

Resources and learning environment	• a selection of relevant literature (both fiction and non-fiction), such as *The Magic School Bus: On the Ocean Floor* by Joanna Cole • access to habitats in the local area, such as gardens, forests, beaches and streams • tool kit for investigations: magnifying glasses, measuring tapes, notebooks, iPads, digital cameras, sketch pencils • videos of different animals in their habitats • access to a range of different local habitats and the animals that live there

Table 5.4   Case study 1: Habitats unit for Year 1 (1 of 5)

STAGE 2: DEVELOPING UNDERSTANDING GOALS

Understanding goal	Level 1	Level 2	Level 3	Level 4
Characteristics of living things	Students **list** the needs of living things.	Students **classify and sort** the needs of living things.	Students **explain** the needs of living things.	Students **connect** the needs of living things and the features of different habitats.
Different habitats and their features	Students **draw and label** different habitats and their features.	Students **explain** the different habitats and their features.	Students **investigate** different habitats and their features.	
How living things interact with their environment	Students **recognise** the interactions between living things and the environment.	Students **make observations** about the interactions between living things and the environment.	Students **analyse** the interactions between living things and the environment.	Students **design** a model showing the interactions between living things and the environment.

Summative assessment idea

- The teacher provides pictures of animals from habitats the class has investigated and asks students to choose one picture to glue into their science notebooks. Each student then draws an appropriate habitat for their chosen animal and labels its food source and shelter.
- The teacher provides pictures of a range of different habitats as well as pictures of a variety of living things. Student have to decide which habitat the living thing belongs in and explain their reasoning.

STAGE 3: DEVELOPING CONCEPTUAL INQUIRY

Step 1: Planning before the unit begins

Inquiry as connection and provocation	**Connections**
	Habitat
	
	- Have students draw their bedroom and the items in it, then compare pictures. The teacher explains that the pictures are different because each bedroom is unique, as it is a representation of your place. The word 'habitat' is introduced.
	- Select picture books about habitats. Using the pictures as a prompt, guide students in a discussion of how they might know whether an animal or plant can be located in a particular area.
	  - What does the animal or plant need to survive?
	  - Is it able to get these things where it lives?
	  - What might make a place unsuitable as a home (too wet, too dry, too cold, too hot)?

Table 5.4   Case study 1: Habitats unit for Year 1 (2 of 5)

Inquiry as connection and provocation *(continued)*	*Needs*
	 • Talk about this concept in terms the students' own lives.
	     • What are your needs for survival?
	     • How are these needs similar to those of other living things?
	 • Introduce the seven needs: grow, move, take in energy (food), make waste, reproduce, breathe, react to things.
	
	 Function
	 • Look at two habitats – for example, the school garden and under the trees.
	     • Observe the living things in these habitats and think about why they might be there.
	     • What does the habitat provide so the living things can survive? How do you know?
	
	 Provocations
	 Students explore different engagements in- and outside the classroom. During the provocations, the teacher observes and records what students say to get a sense of what they understand about the concepts in the unit and therefore what to plan next. The following are some possible provocations for this unit:
	 • Teacher displays pictures or photographs of different habitats, and students work in pairs to record their initial thoughts about what might live there.
	 • Focusing on 3–4 habitats, students use a variety of resources (films, pictures, books, magazines and so on) to make a list of the different features of the habitats and compare them.
	 • Walk, look and sketch: Explore the school grounds, keeping an eye out for any living things that might live there. Encourage students to use their senses and make a note of what they can see, hear, touch, feel and smell.
	 • Allocate small groups an area to visit and re-visit over time to observe the different living things within that particular habitat.

Inquiry as critical wondering	During the initial inquiry as connection and provocation processes and throughout the unit, students' questions will arise. The questions will be recorded as a display titled 'Critical Wonderings'. The questions will be used to guide the teaching and learning.
Step 2: Planning as the unit progresses	
Inquiry as investigation, representation, reflection and transformation	**Needs of living things** • Using the local environment – for example, a park or nature reserve –students collect data by looking for evidence of living things in their habitats. • Have students find evidence of a living thing that lives in a place, such as nests, ant hills, spruce cone piles, droppings, tracks or sounds. Get students to identify the plants and other living things in the same habitat. Students record their findings by drawing a sketch in their science notebooks or using an iPad. • Upon returning to the classroom, students complete a think-pair-share activity with their findings. Students show one another the evidence they found and explain how this evidence might indicate why particular living things can be found in that place. Students then take turns to share their findings and supporting evidence with the whole class.

Table 5.4   Case study 1: Habitats unit for Year 1 (3 of 5)

Inquiry as investigation, representation, reflection and transformation *(continued)*	**Different habitats and their features** • Identify a school garden or an area close to the school that includes a range of different habitats and have students explore and list the different features of each site. The purpose for the investigation is to find out why an animal would choose a particular place for its home. • Students make a detailed representation of their inquiry using drawings, notes and labels. The teacher looks for evidence of understanding that the habitats of living things meet their needs in different ways. **Interactions between living things and the environment** • Students make predictions about where they will find plants and animals and go to a field site to explore and test their predictions. They conduct a detailed investigation of a small section of the field site. Back in the classroom, they share their findings and then make a detailed representation using drawings, notes and labels of the living things in their section and how the living things were interacting in the environment. • Working in groups, students role-play at being scientists or biologists while investigating their area. These investigations can occur over a period of time – for example, over the change of seasons or across a few weeks – so that there is opportunity for the students to observe what grows in the habitat and construct their theories as to why the living things are there. • Students share and compare their findings with other groups. Encourage them to ask questions of the other groups to support and show evidence for how they know why the living things are in their habitat. Monitor the groups and listen for student questions, recording these on poster paper. • After the group presentations there is a short discussion, during which the teacher guides students to think about similarities and differences in living things and habitats.

STAGE 4: EVIDENCE-BASED REFLECTION

What was important about what we did?	• Clarifying the concepts within the unit was important to help the students understand the conceptual focus of the unit. • As the unit was largely hands-on, the level of motivation and engagement indicated that the unit was relevant and intriguing for students. • The natural world is one that is of genuine interest for young children. The students' curiosity was quickly activated with the walks, the observation of living things and the access that students had to the environment. • The wonderings and questions were prompted by the provocations. Students questioned why certain living things reside in one place rather than another and observed that some living things move from place to place for different needs. Deeper complex questions and inquiries were thus evolving. • The viewing of possible habitats before investigations commenced was significant. It was important to also plan the teaching of this unit for the warmer months so that the evidence of living things in habitats was visible.

Table 5.4   Case study 1: Habitats unit for Year 1 (4 of 5)

Did we meet our goals?	• The level of independence of students as inquirers was remarkable throughout the unit. There was a high level of self-management in the group inquiries with respect to the organisation of the tools and materials needed. Opportunity for the development of these skills was a notable element of the unit. • Students' level of understanding about the interaction between living things and the natural environment shifted beyond their initial knowledge base. Some students used the concepts in their explanations in the summative tasks, while others recorded using detailed labelled diagrams.
What changes would we make to the unit?	• It might be beneficial to create some habitats within classrooms or in the playground in addition to what is naturally occurring in the area, such as an ant or worm farm. • Integration with specialist teachers – for example, in the subject of technology – would support the students' field inquiries and add a new dimension to the learning.

Table 5.4   Case study 1: Habitats unit for Year 1 (5 of 5)

CASE STUDY 2
CONSUMER DECISIONS UNIT
YEAR 4

The teacher teams who worked with IGE on this unit (Table 5.5) found that using the template to plan assisted them greatly in understanding the conceptual focus of the unit. Teachers reported that the engagements they planned more effectively met student needs and noted that their lessons were always related to the purpose of the unit.

STAGE 1: DEVELOPING CONCEPTS	
Conceptual understanding	Making informed consumer decisions requires an understanding of the properties of materials and their impact on the environment.
Concepts	• materials • consumerism • sustainability

Understanding goals	Essential questions
Students will understand … • what materials and products are made of • the positive and negative effects of different materials on the environment • how reducing, reusing and recycling materials affects the environment • our role and responsibilities as consumers	• Why is it important to understand what products are made from? • How can we contribute to the sustainability of the environment? • What is our role as consumers?

Table 5.5   Case study 2: Making consumer decisions unit for Year 4 (1 of 6)

Knowledge	Skills
Australian Curriculum: Science Year 4 • Natural and processed materials have a range of physical properties that can influence their use (ACSSU074) • Science knowledge helps people to understand the effect of their actions (ACSHE062) Australian Curriculum: Humanities and Social Sciences Year 4 • The use and management of natural resources and waste, and the different views on how to do this sustainably (ACHASSK090)	Australian Curriculum: Science Year 4 • With guidance, plan and conduct scientific investigations to find answers to questions, considering the safe use of appropriate materials and equipment (ACSIS065) Australian Curriculum: Humanities and Social Sciences Year 4 • Reflect on learning to propose actions in response to an issue or challenge and consider possible effects of proposed actions (ACHASSI081)

Resources and learning environment	• books, films, videos and posters to display in the classroom • measurement tools, such as scales • an exploration table with a variety of products made out of different materials • various items of rubbish (to be collected and displayed as the unit progresses) • access to a local recycling plant

STAGE 2: DEVELOPING UNDERSTANDING GOALS

Understanding goal	Level 1	Level 2	Level 3	Level 4
What materials and products are made of **The positive and negative effects of different materials on the environment**	Students **identify** materials that products are made from and the environmental effect they have.	Students **describe** properties of the materials in products and **categorise** these in connection to the effect they have on the environment.	Students **compare and contrast** properties of the materials in products and **explain** the effect they have on the environment.	Students **analyse** properties of materials in products and **evaluate** the positive and negative effects they have, using evidence and reasoning.
How reducing, reusing and recycling materials affects the environment	Students **state** what reducing, reusing and recycling is.	Students **describe** the differences between reducing, reusing and recycling and the impact they have on the environment.	Students **compare and contrast** reducing, reusing and recycling and **explain** which is the most sustainable.	Students **evaluate** their impact on the environment and **take action** in connection to reusing, recycling and reducing.

Table 5.5   Case study 2: Making consumer decisions unit for Year 4 (2 of 6)

Our role and responsibilities as consumers	Students **state** what a consumer is and **list** basic examples of positive and negative consumer choices.	Students **describe** what positive and negative consumer choices are and provide a range of examples.	Students **explain** what positive and negative consumer choices are and make connections with their own choices.	Students **act** on their understanding of positive and negative consumer choices to make more informed decisions.

Summative assessment ideas

- Students examine a range of different products that are displayed around the classroom. For each product, they answer the following questions:
    - What materials is the product made from?
    - What are the properties of these materials?
    - How do these materials affect the environment?
- In their journals, students record what they purchase, receive and discard over the course of the unit. They identify what materials each item is made from and state what they did with the item once finished using it. At the end of the unit, they evaluate their choices in terms of negative and positive consumer behaviours. They may also evaluate a partner's journal and suggest ways that the other student could make better consumer choices.
- Students complete an audit of the school's reducing, reusing and recycling practices. They create a proposal to improve the school's existing system and present this proposal to a school leader for consideration.

STAGE 3: DEVELOPING CONCEPTUAL INQUIRY

Step 1: Planning before the unit begins

Inquiry as connection and provocation	**Connections**
	
	 Materials
	 • Different materials and products are placed around the room. Students walk around the room and record what they think each material is made of.
	
	 Consumerism
	 • Students record what they buy from the shops for one week. The list is shared with other groups and the question is posed: 'What do we call a person who buys things?' The word 'consumer' is introduced.
	
	 Sustainability
	 • Students are asked to bring in something they own that they have had since they were a baby. Two questions are posed:
	   • Why do you still have it this item?
	   • How has it managed to survive all this time?
	 • The idea of sustainability is introduced and students are provided with other examples of this. They then go for a walk in their immediate environment to look for sustainable and unsustainable practices.

Table 5.5   Case study 2: Making consumer decisions unit for Year 4 (3 of 6)

Inquiry as connection and provocation *(continued)*	**Provocations**
	
	Different stations are set up around the room and students are encouraged to explore. The teacher observes and records what students say to get a sense of what they understand about the unit and therefore what lesson to plan next. Suggested stations include the following:
	
	• Display a time-lapse video of how various products are made. Working in groups, students create a concept board (see p. 85) where they individually write or draw their ideas about the video and then put the main ideas in the middle.
	
	• Students look through different books about recycling, reducing and reusing. On a whiteboard, they draw or write anything they feel is important or want to investigate further.
	
	• Different objects are placed on a table – stationery, plastic toys, food items and so on. Students answer the following questions:
	   • What is the object?
	   • What is the object made of?
	   • What happens to the object when people no longer want to use it?

Inquiry as critical wondering	As a part of inquiry as connection and provocation and throughout the unit, students' questions will arise. The questions will be recorded as a display titled 'Critical Wonderings'. The questions will be used to guide the teaching and learning.
	**Step 2: Planning as the unit progresses**
Inquiry as investigation, representation, reflection and transformation	**What materials and products are made of and the positive and negative impact of materials on the environment** • Experiments are set up to see which materials are biodegradable and which ones are not. This can be completed over the course of the unit, with students keeping observational journals to record their findings. • Pictures and videos of waste products such as landfill are displayed. Students use a chart to record what the materials are, whether those materials have a negative impact on the environment when discarded and what they or others could do to reduce this impact. • Students perform an individual inquiry by choosing a material and investigating its impact on the environment. • As a class, students create a factual text or video that explains the impact different materials have on the environment. • Different statements about materials and waste are given to the students and they have to decide if the statements are true or false. **How reducing, reusing and recycling materials affects the environment** • Throughout the unit, statements about sustainability are collected, and these are ranked at a later date using a diamond display (see p. 83). • Students go on excursions to various recycling plants to learn about recycling. • Students choose a product and write a procedural text about the process that the product goes through when recycled. • Different products are placed on the table and students categorise them based on whether they can be recycled, reused or reduced.

Table 5.5   Case study 2: Making consumer decisions unit for Year 4 (4 of 6)

Inquiry as investigation, representation, reflection and transformation *(continued)*	• Each day, students collect the garbage they throw out and weigh it. They record the data. Over the weeks, they try to reduce the waste they produce, stating how they plan to do this and weighing their daily waste to check their progress. • Students audit their own home in terms of how effectively they reduce, reuse and recycle. They develop suggestions on how they could improve this. • Students write a persuasive text stating why they think it is important to recycle reuse and reduce. • Questions about reducing, reusing and recycling are written on large sheets of paper. Students record their ideas as a group and, when prompted by the teacher, move to the next question. Students cannot repeat what previous groups have written. **The role of a consumer and how to make informed consumer decisions** • Students record what they purchase each day of the unit. They look at their consumer choices as the unit progresses and decide if they were good or bad consumer choices and why. • Students read scenarios about consumer choices and do a diamond display (see p. 83) to order the scenarios from the best consumer choices to the worst consumer choices. • Using shopping bags, the teacher puts a variety of products into the bags; each bag should contain different products. The full shopping bags are placed on different tables. For each bag, students work in groups and have to decide if the shopper made good or bad consumer choices, giving reasons for their assessment. They then decide which shopper made the best consumer choices overall. Their findings are shared with the rest of the class.

STAGE 4: EVIDENCE-BASED REFLECTION	
What was important about what we did?	• The provocations gave us a chance to see what students' current level of understanding was. From the misconceptions that arose, it became clear that we needed to spend more time focusing on the different materials that products are made from. • The students really enjoyed looking at consumer choices. The hands-on aspect of it promoted engagement, and the debates around what is or isn't a good consumer choice were great. We felt that by having students defend their point of view, they developed an even better understanding of the concepts. • The students had to present to the principal their ideas for improvement across the school. During their practice, it was clear that we needed to develop criteria on what makes a good presentation. We therefore changed the direction of the unit a bit to spend time on developing these skills so that the presentation could be successful.
Did we meet our goals?	• The majority of students were successful in the summative assessment tasks. The levels of understanding helped us to pinpoint where students were at in their current understanding. • We feel that the students have mastered the knowledge component of the unit and are pleased with the tasks we developed to enable this to occur.

Table 5.5   Case study 2: Making consumer decisions unit for Year 4 (5 of 6)

| What changes would we make to the unit? | • Next time, we would think more about the resources used to support the unit. It was difficult to find resources that were at an appropriate level for the students. We feel that if we were to be a bit more selective with the materials, it would be easier to determine whether our resources were age-appropriate prior to starting the unit. |
| | • We would also ensure that we spent a bit more time front-loading students with the skills they need. For example, some students had difficulty working with iPads, so next time we would run small instructional groups to make sure all students have the required skills. |

Table 5.5 Case study 2: Making consumer decisions unit for Year 4 (6 of 6)

CASE STUDY 3
INDIGENOUS CULTURES UNIT
YEAR 6

Previously in this unit (Table 5.6, pp. 70–75), the teachers and students looked at indigenous peoples by researching an indigenous culture. The teachers wanted to open up the unit by looking at how indigenous cultures have or have not changed and getting students compare and contrast their findings. They also wanted to move away from content towards a more conceptually focused unit.

This unit was not developed using the Australian Curriculum; rather, it was developed with teachers at an international school. Nevertheless, this unit is just as relevant in Australia and could take more of a national perspective, with a greater focus on Aboriginal and Torres Strait Islander Peoples.

STAGE 1: DEVELOPING CONCEPTS		
Conceptual understanding	Examining evidence of indigenous cultures provides insight into their past and present.	
Concepts	• evidence • culture • indigenous • cause and effect	
Understanding goals		Essential questions
• what evidence can tell us about indigenous cultures • the connections between indigenous peoples and their places • the connections between the past and present of indigenous cultures		• What is an indigenous culture? • How and why have indigenous cultures changed? • What is evidence, and how can we best use evidence to support our findings?

Table 5.6 Case study 3: Indigenous cultures unit for Year 6 (1 of 6)

Knowledge	Skills
Australian Curriculum: Humanities and Social Sciences Year 6 • The contribution of individuals and groups to the development of Australian society since Federation (ACHASSK137) • The world's cultural diversity, including that of its indigenous peoples (ACHASSK140) • The effects that people's connections with, and proximity to, places throughout the world have on shaping their awareness and opinion of those places (ACHASSK142) Australian Curriculum: Visual Arts Years 5 and 6 • Explain how visual arts conventions communicate meaning by comparing artworks from different social, cultural and historical contexts, including Aboriginal and Torres Strait Islander artworks (ACAVAR117) Australian Curriculum: Health and Physical Education Years 5 and 6 • Examine how identities are influenced by people and places (ACPPS051)	Australian Curriculum: Humanities and Social Sciences Year 6 • Develop appropriate questions to guide an inquiry about people, events, developments, places, systems and challenges (ACHASSI122) • Locate and collect relevant information and data from primary and secondary sources (ACHASSI123) • Sequence information about people's lives, events, developments and phenomena using a variety of methods including timelines (ACHASSI125) • Examine primary and secondary sources to determine their origin and purpose (ACHASSI126) • Examine different viewpoints on actions, events, issues and phenomena in the past and present (ACHASSI127) • Evaluate evidence to draw conclusions (ACHASSI129) • Work in groups to generate responses to issues and challenges (ACHASSI130)
Resources and learning environment	• TED Talks • books, artefacts and pictures connected to indigenous cultures • *National Geographic* magazines • pictures and videos depicting changes in indigenous cultures

STAGE 2: DEVELOPING UNDERSTANDING GOALS

Understanding goal	Level 1	Level 2	Level 3	Level 4
What evidence can tell us about indigenous cultures	Students **recall** various evidence and what it may say about indigenous cultures.	Students **describe** various evidence, and **make inferences** about what it reveals about indigenous cultures.	Students **compare and contrast** various items of evidence and make generalisations about indigenous cultures.	Students **assess** the validity of various items of evidence and **make detailed inferences** about indigenous cultures.

Table 5.6　Case study 3: Indigenous cultures unit for Year 6 (2 of 6)

The connections between indigenous peoples and their places	Students **recall** the connections between a place and the culture of its people.	Students **explain** the connections between a place and the culture of its people, including connections to beliefs and values.	Students **compare and contrast** the connections between a place and the culture of its people, **explaining** the impact beliefs and values have on these.	Students **analyse** the connections between a place and the culture of its people, **evaluating** cultural beliefs and values and how they have shaped the place.
The connections between the past and present of indigenous cultures	Students **state** the changes that have occurred in some indigenous cultures and why.	Students **describe** the changes that have occurred in some indigenous cultures and **explain** why some have changed over time while others have not.	Students **explain** the changes that have occurred in some indigenous cultures, **making comparisons** to determine why these changes have or have not occurred.	Students **analyse** the changes that have occurred in some indigenous cultures, **evaluating** why some have changed over time while others have not. They use a range of evidence to back up their conclusions.

Summative assessment ideas
• Students create an artwork that is representative of their understanding of an indigenous culture. • Students create a museum connected to an indigenous culture. In the museum, they use a variety of evidence and state clearly what the evidence tells them with regard to beliefs, values and changes in the indigenous culture. • Students go to a museum, learn about different indigenous cultures and then use a concept map (see p. 52) to explain the connections between culture, indigenous peoples and change. This is followed by a interview with the teacher to determine how much the student has understood.

STAGE 3: DEVELOPING CONCEPTUAL INQUIRY
Step 1: Planning before the unit begins

Inquiry as connection and provocation	**Connections** *Evidence* Students bring in an item from home that they feel represents something about themselves. These are shared in small groups. Students guess what each item might mean, and at the end of the discussion the person to whom each item belongs explains its meaning. The word 'evidence' is introduced, and the students are asked, 'What did you learn about this person from the evidence presented?'

Table 5.6   Case study 3: Indigenous cultures unit for Year 6 (3 of 6)

Inquiry as connection and provocation *(continued)*	*Culture*
	Students ask their parents about what their culture is. They bring back their ideas and do a class concept board (p. 85) as a way to share what they all know and look for similarities and differences.
	
	Indigenous
	Pictures of indigenous animals and plants are placed around the room as a rotation. Students record where the animals and plants come from and why. The word 'indigenous' is introduced, and a class definition is developed: 'native to a particular place'.
	
	Cause and effect
	A book connected to the unit is read to the students. At the end of the story, students do a cause-and-effect chart based on their ideas from the book. They then define what 'cause and effect' means to them.
	
	Provocations
	A series of rotations is used to find out what students know already and to provoke their curiosity about the unit. Provocations could include the following:
	
	• pictures of indigenous people and cultures. Students complete a Frayer model (see pp. 84–85) around the word 'culture'.
	• artefacts connected to indigenous cultures. Students fill in a chart to answer the following questions:
	    • What do you think it is?
	    • Where do you think it came from?
	    • How do you know?

Inquiry as critical wondering	Through different learning engagements, students will be asked to note down their questions. The questions will be written and collected on sticky notes. Students will sort the questions throughout the unit, and these will be used to • plan for further learning engagements that will assist in answering the questions • be used as a part of the museum project on indigenous cultures
	**Step 2: Planning as the unit progresses**
Inquiry as investigation, representation, reflection and transformation	**What evidence can tell us about indigenous cultures** • During their excursion to the museum, students look at the different artefacts and, in their journals, make inferences about what the evidence tells them about indigenous cultures. This is shared back at school, and the students create a concept map (p. 52) based on their understanding. • Place different types of evidence on tables and have students decide if the evidence is a primary source or a secondary source. Have them define what a primary or secondary source of evidence is. • Students take on different roles – for example, archaeologist or historian – and explain an artefact from that perspective. • In groups, students choose an indigenous culture to learn more about. They pose questions about what they want to know. • Students interpret indigenous artwork connected to the unit.

Table 5.6 Case study 3: Indigenous cultures unit for Year 6 (4 of 6)

Inquiry as investigation, representation, reflection and transformation (continued)	**The connections between indigenous people and their places**
	• Students go for a walk around their environment while thinking about the following questions:
	   • How does our environment affect the way we live?
	   • What do the buildings in the environment tell us about the way local people live their lives?
	• Students are given images of different environments where indigenous people live. They rotate around the different environments, thinking about the following questions:
	   • What does this environment tell us about how people live?
	   • How might this environment affect the way you live your life?
	• Students look through books, watch videos and examine artefacts to make inferences about the connection between the places that indigenous peoples live, their ways of life and their beliefs and values. They compare and contrast the similarities and differences between cultures.
	• Students interview an indigenous person about their cultural connections to their place and how their place impacts on the way they live.
	The connections between the past and present of indigenous cultures
	• The teacher poses the question, 'Do you think indigenous peoples live their life today like they did 100 years ago? Why? Why not?' Working in groups, students record their ideas on a concept board (see p. 85).
	• Show a video about an indigenous culture that explains how that culture has changed over time. At the end, get students in groups to draw a story map stating what has changed, and have them write below it why they think those changes occurred. The students share their story maps and start to build an understanding of what causes changes in indigenous cultures.
	• Show a video about an indigenous culture that has not changed over time, and ask students to think about the following:
	   • What did you see?
	   • What do you think?
	   • Why do you think it is the way it is?
	• In groups, students choose an indigenous culture to learn more about. They pose their own questions and state where they will gather their evidence. This will lead into the museum display for the summative assessment.

STAGE 4: EVIDENCE-BASED REFLECTION

What was important about what we did?	• The connections to the concepts and provocations helped to get the students interested in the unit. The use of real artefacts and having these in the classroom promoted ongoing learning throughout the unit. • Going to the museum worked well, as it enabled students to see a greater variety of artefacts, and having them take pictures enabled them to recall aspects they had forgotten.

Table 5.6   Case study 3: Indigenous cultures unit for Year 6 (5 of 6)

What was important about what we did? *(continued)*	• The museum project really engaged the students. We noticed that students were spending an enormous amount of time trying to work out exactly what to put in their museums. As a consequence of this, the class developed criteria on what makes a good exhibit in a museum, which greatly assisted them with their displays. The groups used the criteria to evaluate each other's displays.
	• The ongoing collection of student questions enabled us to get a clear picture of what they did not understand and what they were interested in. These questions were incorporated into the learning engagements, and they were also used in the interviews and when examining an indigenous culture for the museum.
Did we meet our goals?	• Students were able to articulate their understanding at some level of the understanding goals.
	• The knowledge component was covered through the various learning engagements, particularly the interview.
	• It was difficult to find resources to address some of the geographical skills we identified, so we feel that this goal was not met.
	• The students were engaged in the unit, and the learning that took place enabled them to see different perspectives and gain new insights.
What changes would we make to the unit?	• We would make sure that we have more artefacts that connect to indigenous cultures. We will start to build up these resources for when we teach the unit again.
	• It was difficult to find time to interview each student. Next time, we will pose questions to students first and have them make a concept map (see p. 52) to answer the questions prior to the interview. That way, they will come to the conference more prepared and it will not take as long.

Table 5.6   Case study 3: Indigenous cultures unit for Year 6 (6 of 6)

CASE STUDY 4
FORCES AND MOTION UNIT
YEAR 4

In discussions for this unit (Table 5.7, pp. 76–80), teachers quickly realised that subject knowledge is critical for conceptual understanding and inquiry. Upon using the IGE planning template, they found that clarifying the understanding goals and explicitly stating the overarching conceptual understanding gave the unit a cohesive direction in terms of science knowledge and concepts.

The assessment rubric for levels of understanding took time to develop, as it required the teachers to investigate for themselves ideas around forces and motion that would be compelling and significant for their students.

IGE has developed this unit with teachers in both international and Australian school settings. Since forces and motion is a fundamental topic of science instruction, the unit can be adapted to work with any curriculum.

STAGE 1: DEVELOPING CONCEPTS	
Conceptual understanding	Physical forces affect the way people live and how the world works.
Concepts	<ul><li>force</li><li>motion</li><li>variables</li><li>application</li></ul>

Understanding goals	Essential questions
<ul><li>forces exist in the physical world</li><li>forces and motion inform technological innovation</li><li>the design cycle and its application to real-life situations</li></ul>	<ul><li>How are forces and motion connected?</li><li>How do forces affect the motion of an object?</li><li>How is energy conserved?</li><li>How is changing technology changing society?</li></ul>

Knowledge	Skills
Australian Curriculum: Science Year 4<ul><li>Forces can be exerted by one object on another through direct contact or from a distance (ACSSU076)</li><li>Science involves making predictions and describing patterns and relationships (ACSHE061)</li><li>Science knowledge helps people to understand the effect of their actions (ACSHE062)</li></ul>Australian Curriculum: Design and Technologies Years 3 and 4<ul><li>Investigate how forces and the properties of materials affect the behaviour of a product or system (ACTDEK011)</li></ul>	Australian Curriculum: Science Year 4<ul><li>With guidance, identify questions in familiar contexts that can be investigated scientifically and make predictions based on prior knowledge (ACSIS064)</li><li>With guidance, plan and conduct scientific investigations to find answers to questions, considering the safe use of appropriate materials and equipment (ACSIS065)</li><li>Represent and communicate observations, ideas and findings using formal and informal representations (ACSIS071)</li></ul>Australian Curriculum: Design and Technologies Years 3 and 4<ul><li>Critique needs or opportunities for designing and explore and test a variety of materials, components, tools and equipment and the techniques needed to produce designed solutions (ACTDEP014)</li><li>Generate, develop, and communicate design ideas and decisions using appropriate technical terms and graphical representation techniques (ACTDEP015)</li><li>Select and use materials, components, tools and equipment using safe work practices to make designed solutions (ACTDEP016)</li></ul>

Table 5.7 Case study 4: Forces and motion unit for Year 4 (1 of 5)

Resources and learning environment	• a range of materials to support the unit, including videos and non-fiction texts • guest speakers from the design industry • a selection of artefacts that can be used for provocations • areas in the classroom that provide ready access to the materials and tools needed for investigations • key language and scientific principles accessible to the students to support their ongoing conceptual understanding of the unit

STAGE 2: DEVELOPING UNDERSTANDING GOALS

Understanding goal	Level 1	Level 2	Level 3	Level 4
Forces exist in the physical world	**Observe, sketch** and **label** different examples of forces on the motion and energy of an object.	**Explain** how forces causes motion or energy.	**Investigate** the effect of several forces on the motion and energy of an object.	**Design** an application to show how knowledge of forces and energy informs technological innovation.
Forces and motion inform technological innovation	**Identify** how knowledge of forces and motion informs technological innovation.	**Make observations** about how knowledge of forces and motion informs technological innovation.	**Explain** how knowledge of forces and motion informs technological innovation.	**Apply** the concepts using knowledge of the design cycle and its application to real-life situations.
The design cycle and its application to real-life situations	**Illustrate** the design cycle and its application to real-life situations.	**Explain** the design cycle and its application to real-life situations.	**Investigate** using the design cycle and its application to real-life situations.	

Summative assessment ideas

- Other-worldly sports: Students create a poster illustrating how their favourite sport might look on a planet of their choosing, explaining how differences in gravity and atmosphere could affect the forces on players and their equipment.
- Newtonian vehicle: Design and build a self-propelling vehicle, including schematics showing the forces on the stationary and moving vehicle and a written explanation of how the vehicle demonstrates Newton's laws.

Table 5.7   Case study 4: Forces and motion unit for Year 4 (2 of 5)

STAGE 3: DEVELOPING LEARNING ENGAGEMENTS	
Step 1: Planning before the unit begins	
Inquiry as connection and provocation	**Connections** *Force* • Explain to the students what 'force' is and whether the word has the same meaning in science as in everyday life. A concept wall (see p. 83) is then used to visually collect questions, wonderings and reflections. • Students engage in hands-on guided inquiries that explore the idea of force – for instance, by pulling a card out from under a coin to illustrate inertia. *Motion* • Introduce the principles of Newton's laws of motion through the use of easily understandable material. Gravity and friction are just two of the forces used. • Students who are at beginning levels of understanding can be involved in free play with forces and motion, while more advanced students can study applied physics through a computer simulation. *Variables* • Set up open inquiry opportunities that involve fair testing, constants and controlled variables. Following this, introduce the idea that variables are conditions that can be changed and that can affect outcomes. • Introduce the scientific terms that describe the concept of variables, such as size, shape, temperature, amount, volume and rate. *Application* • Using a range of real-life examples where force and motion are been applied, get students to look, watch, listen and then represent what they have seen. **Provocations** Different stations are set up for students to rotate through while the teacher records what students say to get a sense of what to plan next. This evidence can be gathered using a whole-class concept wall (see p. 83) along with students' science journals.
Inquiry as critical wondering	As a part of inquiry as connection and provocation and throughout the unit, students' questions will arise. The questions will be recorded as a display titled 'Critical Wonderings'. The questions will be used to guide the teaching and learning.
Step 2: Planning as the unit progresses	
Inquiry as investigation, representation, reflection and transformation	Throughout the unit, students keep a science journal, which they use to observe and record the scientific process as they construct meaning. Students record their thinking and responses as personal connections are made, using methods such as observational sketches, photographs of the process and ongoing written reflections. **Forces exist in the physical world** • Introduce the 5Es of scientific inquiry: engage, explore, explain, elaborate and evaluate. • Introduce Newton's three laws of motion to describe how physical objects move and how forces affect their motion. Plan a range of investigations for students to experience Newton's laws in action through hands-on activities.

Table 5.7   Case study 4: Forces and motion unit for Year 4 (3 of 5)

Inquiry as investigation, representation, reflection and transformation *(continued)*	<ul><li>Newton's First Law of Motion: According to Newton's first law of motion, an object stays at rest or keeps moving at the same speed unless a force makes it change its motion. To clarify how Newton's first law works for things in motion, explain that friction is a force.</li><li>Newton's Second Law of Motion: According to Newton's second law of motion, force applied to an object makes it move faster; the greater the force, the faster the object speeds up. To show the second law of motion in action, have the children hit balls of different sizes with bats and note how hard they are hitting and how fast the ball moves.</li><li>Newton's Third Law of Motion: Newton's third law states that every action has an equal and opposite reaction. To demonstrate, let air out of an inflated balloon and explain how this is similar to the way rockets are launched upwards by pushing hot gases out and downwards.</li></ul><ul><li>In all investigations, explore the concept of variables.<ul><li>Compare variables of the same type, such as different surfaces with different shapes and properties.</li><li>Combine variables to see if there are patterns or relationships to use as explanations – for instance, variables that affect energy transfer.</li><li>Identify variables and describe how they operate to affect other variables.</li></ul></li></ul>**Forces and motion inform technological innovation, and the design cycle and its application to real-life situations**<ul><li>Provide opportunities for students to design and test their own innovations using the principles of Newton's laws. Students use the design cycle to apply the concepts of force and motion, changing only one variable at a time in a controlled experiment, then use experimental results to predict outcomes of future experiments.</li><li>Use the following questions to support students in their design process:<ul><li>What makes a good scientific question?</li><li>How do scientific questions drive the inquiry process?</li><li>What is a fair test?</li><li>What steps do I need to take to test my question?</li></ul></li></ul>

STAGE 4: EVIDENCE-BASED REFLECTION	
What was important about what we did?	<ul><li>For students, the opportunity to make sense of forces and motion in real-world contexts provided a tangible context for the scientific principles. Through provocations and making connections, students immediately developed a genuine interest in the theories, especially Newton's laws. Previously, many of these scientific principles had seemed quite abstract to students, but the more hands-on investigative approach opened possibilities for theorising and predicting using real-world application.</li><li>The other important aspect of this unit was its clear focus on the language of science. Taking time to draw out the meanings of the concepts was critical in informing more effective questioning and wondering by the students.</li></ul>

Table 5.7   Case study 4: Forces and motion unit for Year 4 (4of 5)

Did we meet our goals?	• Throughout the unit, the teachers spent a lot of time clarifying their own science knowledge. This was important to ensure that the time being allocated to investigation was science-driven, and it also provided rich contexts for scientific understanding. The expectations for the unit were met, with some students being able to articulate and explain concepts more effectively, while others were able to provide diagrams that explained the scientific principles. • The open-ended investigations offered the chance for students to experiment with diverse approaches, which was significant in building on prior and developing knowledge. • The use of the design cycle challenged the students in their application of science skills.
What changes would we make to the unit?	• It might be good to spend a little more time expanding on the science concepts prior to shifting into the investigation and transformation phase of the unit. There was a need for considerable scaffolding throughout the process, which we felt to suggest that more time should be dedicated connection and provocation.

Table 5.7   Case study 4: Forces and motion unit for Year 4 (3 of 5)

APPENDIX: STRATEGIES FOR CONCEPTUAL LEARNING

In order to shift from content to concept-based lesson planning, educators need cognitive strategies that introduce the concept explicitly and explore it in depth. Effective learning strategies assist the learner to create connections with existing knowledge and enable the educator to identify any misconceptions that may exist.

The following are specific cognitive strategies that we recommend for teachers of conceptual learning. Please note that these are only some of the many possibilities for conceptual instruction, and teachers are encouraged to seek out or devise their own activities in response to their students' particular needs.

- **Sketch the concept.** On a blank piece of paper, students create a sketch that visually represents their understanding of the concept. This representation may be literal or abstract, but it should include pictures only – no words. Once they have finished, each student displays their sketch for their peers and asks them to speculate on the reasoning behind it.

- **Concept categorisation.** On sticky notes, each student writes down all of the ideas they have about the concept, using a new note for each idea. Students are not allowed to talk to one another during this time. Each individual places their ideas in the middle of the table, and the students work as a group to sort and classify the ideas they have about the concept. They may add or take away some of the ideas presented. Once they have categorised their ideas, the students write new headings for each concept category.

- **Freeze frame.** A 'freeze frame' is when students create a human photo by using their bodies to construct a tableau. Students work in groups to create a freeze frame that shows their understanding of the concept.

- **Concept die.** One question related to the the concept is written on each section of the die template in Figure A.1 (p. 82), available for download at **go.hbe.com.au**). In groups, students roll the die and answer the question that comes up. Suggested questions include the following:

  - What is the concept?
  - How does the concept work?
  - Why do we need to know about the concept?

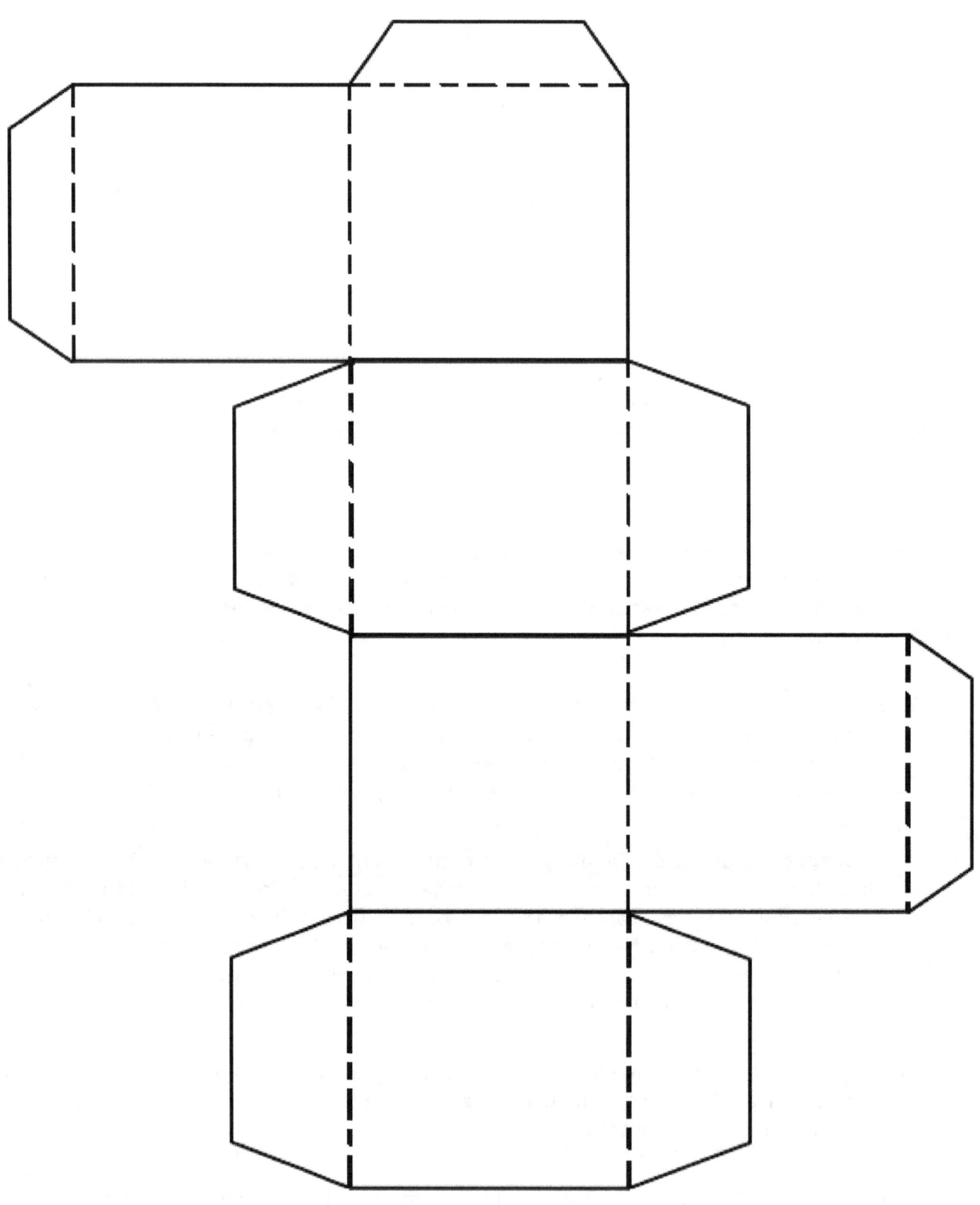

Figure A.1   Concept die

- Does the concept change in different situations?
- How does the concept connect to your own life?
- What is the most important thing to understand about the concept?

↘ **Pass-it-on.** The teacher writes several questions about the concept on large sheets of paper. Students work in groups to answer the questions, writing as much as they can. The teacher then says 'Pass' and the paper is passed to the next group, who read what was written and add more ideas. This continues until each group has their original piece of paper back. The idea is that each time students have to add to others' responses, they are made to think more deeply about their own view of the concept.

↘ **Concept walk.** The teacher places around the classroom a variety of words, objects, photos, pictures and ideas that relate to the concept. Students walk around the room looking at these items and record the ideas and thoughts about the concept that arise from their walk.

↘ **Concept headline.** The teacher prompts students to display their understanding of the concept by asking, 'If you were to write a headline that captures what is most important about the concept, what would that headline be?' Follow-up questions can then be asked to probe how students' ideas about the concept have changed over the course of the unit: 'How has your headline changed based on today's discussion? How does it differ from what you would have said yesterday?' (adapted from Visible Thinking n.d.b).

↘ **Diamond display.** Prepare a set of nine different statements or opinions about the concept. The statements should vary in point of view and, if possible, incorporate various generalisations that students themselves have made about the concept. Each statement should be written on its own square of paper.

Once the statements have been handed out, students work either in small groups or individually to arrange them in a diamond shape. The statement at the top is the one they agree with the most. The next line has two statements, then three, then another two, all arranged in order of priority until the last statement – the one they least agree with – is placed at the bottom. The resulting diamond is shared with others, and students are given the opportunity to justify their opinions.

↘ **True/false/not sure.** Working individually or in small groups, students are given statements relating to the concept. They have to decide if the statements are true or false and state why they think this, then they discuss their reasoning in comparison with that of others.

↘ **Concept wall.** The concept is written in the centre of a sheet of poster paper and hung on the wall. Throughout the unit, students can add ideas and statements about the concept, draw pictures related to the concept, find and place pictures related to the concept, write words related to the concept and post questions that they have about the concept. This enables the teacher to gain an understanding of what students do or do not know, in this way functioning as a formative tool throughout the unit.

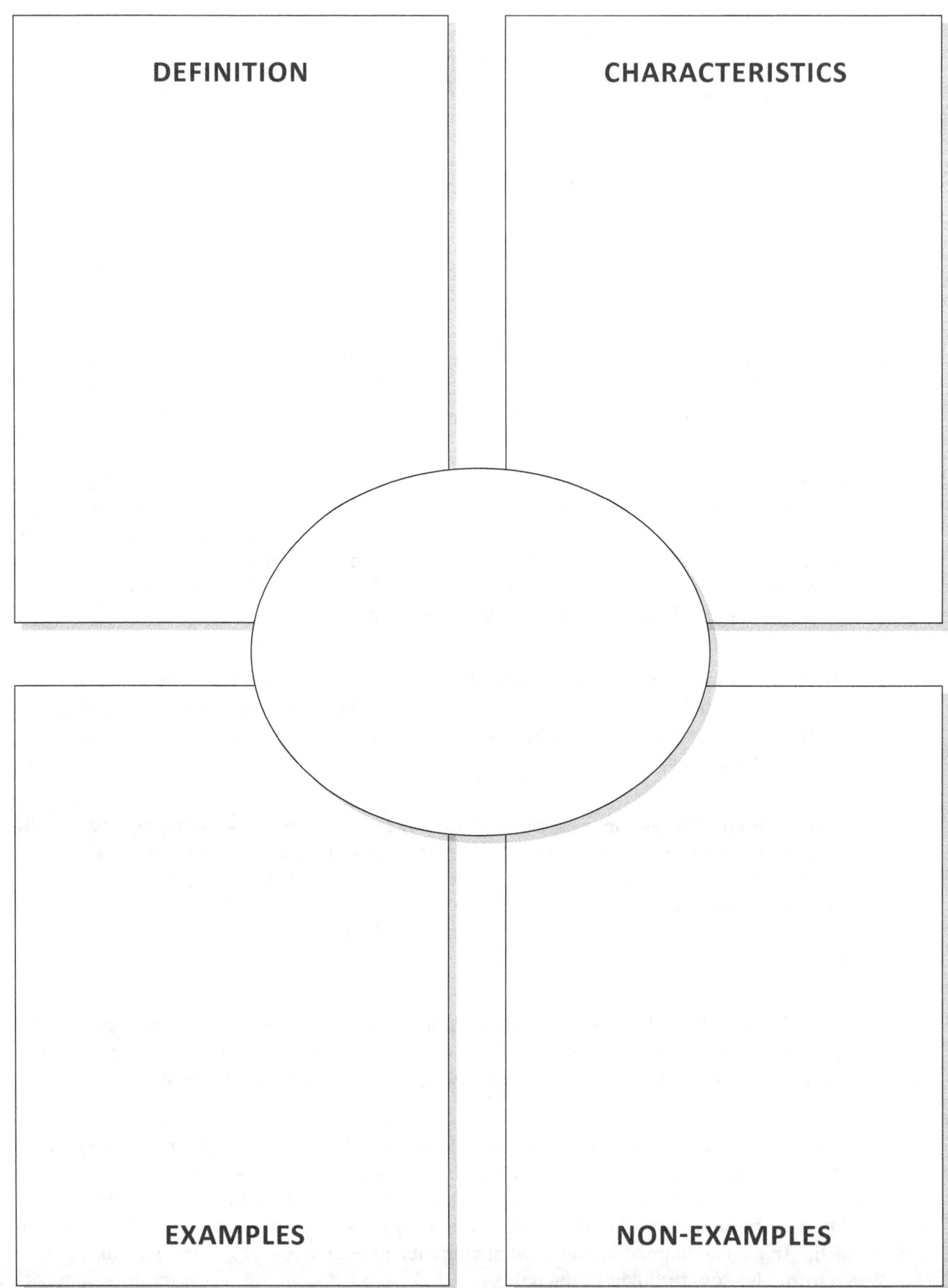

DEFINITION

CHARACTERISTICS

EXAMPLES

NON-EXAMPLES

Figure A.2   Frayer Concept Chart

- **Concept board.** Students form groups of four. They write the concept as a heading in the middle of a sheet of poster paper. Each student takes one quarter of the page and silently writes or sketches their ideas about the concept – as few or as many as they feel to be necessary. Once they have done this, each individual shares their ideas, and those on which the whole group agrees are placed in the middle under the heading of the concept word. This activity gives students the chance to share ideas and reflect on their understanding of the concept with their peers.

- **Frayer concept chart.** The Frayer conceptual model can be used to assess student's ongoing development of their understanding of the concept. Students can fill it in towards the beginning of the unit and revisit it throughout the unit.

  Using the downloadable template provided (Figure A.2), students write the concept in the middle and then record what they understand about the concept in relation to each section.

  - Definition: Students write a definition of the concept.
  - Characteristics: Students list the characteristics of the concept
  - Examples: Students write actual examples related to the concept.
  - Non-examples: Students write what the concept isn't.

- **Exit slips.** Teachers hand out exit cards with reflective prompts for students. The downloadable template in Figure A.3 (p. 86) gives four examples, but there are many more possibilities. Students fill in their exit cards just prior to leaving the lesson or finishing for the day.

- **Connect, extend, challenge.** This is a useful questioning strategy for connecting new ideas to prior knowledge. Teachers ask the following four questions:

  - How are the ideas and information presented connected to what you already knew?
  - What new ideas did you get that extended or pushed your thinking in new directions?
  - What is still challenging or confusing for you to get your mind around? (adapted from Visible Thinking n.d.a).

- **Reflective journal.** Students keep a regular journal in which they record their ongoing ideas and thoughts about the concept. Teachers may want to monitor the journals to keep track of how student learning evolves throughout the unit.

- **Turn and talk.** Students turn to the person next to them and state everything that they understand about a given concept. Next, they tell their partner something that they want to know more about in connection with a concept.

- **I used to think … but now I think …** Students reflect on their previous understanding and how it has changed. They state what it was they used to think and explain how the new learning has made them rethink their previously held ideas.

EXIT CARD

Name _____

What do you now understand about the concept?

What are you still trying to understand about the concept?

What is the most important thing that you have learnt about the concept?

EXIT CARD

Name _____

Three things I have learnt about the concept …

Two things I found interesting about the concept …

One thing I still want to know about the concept …

EXIT CARD

Name _____

I was surprised to learn …

I will always remember …

I'm still now sure about …

EXIT CARD

Name _____

I get it!

I don't get it …

Figure A.3   Concept exit cards

REFERENCES

ACARA (Australian Curriculum, Assessment and Reporting Authority) 2015, Australian Curriculum v8, http://www.australiancurriculum.edu.au

Adoniou, M, Louden, B, Zyngier, D & Riddle, S 2014 (12 October), 'National curriculum review: Experts respond', *The Conversation*, http://theconversation.com/national-curriculum-review-experts-respond-26913

Askell-Williams, H 2014, 'Students' use of good quality learning strategies: A multilevel model of change over five years of secondary school', ACER (Australian Council for Educational Research), http://research.acer.edu.au/cgi/viewcontent.cgi?article=1235&context=research_conference

Bransford, JD, Brown AL & Cocking RR (eds) 2000, *How people learn: Brain, mind, experience and school*, rev. edn, National Academy Press, Washington, USA.

Blythe, T & Associates 1998, *Teaching for understanding guide*, Jossey-Bass, San Francisco.

Bruner, J 1960, *The process of education*, Harvard University Press, Cambridge, USA.

Bruner, J, Goodnow, JJ & Austin, GA 2009 (1956), *A study of thinking*, rev. edn, Transaction Publishers, New Brunswick, USA.

Dunlosky, J 2013, 'Strengthening the student toolbox: Study strategies to boost learning', *American Educator*, vol. 37, no. 3, http://www.aft.org/sites/default/files/periodicals/dunlosky.pdf

Erickson, HL 2007, *Concept-based curriculum and instruction: Teaching beyond the facts*, Hawker Brownlow Education, Melbourne.

Erickson, HL 2008, *Stirring the head, heart and soul: Redefining curriculum, instruction and content-based learning*, 3rd edn, Hawker Brownlow Education, Melbourne.

Greenville County Schools n.d., 'Essential questions', http://greenville.k12.sc.us/league/esques.html

Heick, T 2014 (16 October), 'A giant list of really good essential questions', *TeachThought* (blog), http://www.teachthought.com/learning/examples-of-essential-question

'In the Know: Are our children learning enough about whales?' 2008, YouTube video, *The Onion*, https://www.youtube.com/watch?v=POi4rvN_Yts

McCoy, JD & Ketterlin-Geller, LR 2004, 'Rethinking instructional delivery for diverse student populations', *Intervention in School and Clinic*, vol. 40, no. 2, http://www.researchgate.net/profile/Leanne_Ketterlin_Geller/publication/240730835_Rethinking_Instructional_Delivery_for_Diverse_Student_PopulationsServing_All_Learners_with_Concept-Based_Instruction/links/547d0b8a0cf27ed9786231bb.pdf

Piaget, J 1928, *The child's conception of the world*, Routledge and Kegan Paul, London.

Small, MK 2013, *Good questions: Great ways to differentiate mathematics instruction*, 2nd edn, Hawker Brownlow Education, Melbourne.

Student Achievement Division 2011, 'Asking effective questions', Ontario Ministry of Education, http://www.edu.gov.on.ca/eng/literacynumeracy/inspire/research/cbs_askingeffectivequestions.pdf

Téllez, K 2014, 'Teaching facts, skills, concepts, and morals: What's the difference?' University of California, Santa Cruz, http://people.ucsc.edu/~ktellez/facts-skills-con.html

Through these eyes 2004, motion picture, directed by Charles Laird, National Film Board of Canada, https://www.nfb.ca/film/through_these_eyes

Treadwell, M 2008, *The conceptual age and the revolution: Schoolv2.0*, Hawker Brownlow Education, Melbourne.

Visible Thinking n.d.a, 'Connect extend challenge', Harvard Graduate School of Education, http://www.visiblethinkingpz.org/VisibleThinking_html_files/03_ThinkingRoutines/03d_UnderstandingRoutines/ConnectExtendChallenge/ConnectExtend_Routine.html

Visible Thinking n.d.b, 'Headlines', Harvard Graduate School of Education, http://www.visiblethinkingpz.org/VisibleThinking_html_files/03_ThinkingRoutines/03d_UnderstandingRoutines/Headlines/Headlines_Routine.html

Visible Thinking n.d.c, 'I used to think ... But now I think ...', Harvard Graduate School of Education, http://www.visiblethinkingpz.org/VisibleThinking_html_files/03_ThinkingRoutines/03c_Core_routines/UsedToThink/UsedToThink_Routine.htm

Visible Thinking n.d.d, 'What makes you say that', http://www.visiblethinkingpz.org/VisibleThinking_html_files/03_ThinkingRoutines/03d_UnderstandingRoutines/WhatMakes/WhatMakes_Routine.html

Webb, NL 2002 (28 March), 'Depth-of-knowledge levels for four content areas', http://schools.nyc.gov/NR/rdonlyres/2711181C-2108-40C4-A7F8-76F243C9B910/0/DOKFourContentAreas.pdf

ACKNOWLEDGEMENTS

IGE would like to recognise the contributions made to *Taking the Complexity out of Concepts* by Nicole Ginnane, who has helped IGE to understand the research and history of conceptual learning and its significance for learners. Nicole has contributed her ideas and thoughts throughout the book, and we are grateful for her critical eye, questioning and perspective. Her input has been invaluable.

IGE would also like to thank the schools with whom we have worked during the development of *Taking the Complexity out of Concepts*. These schools provided us with the opportunity to trial and implement our models, and their ongoing reflections have contributed greatly to the book:

- ⬊ Anglo-American School of Moscow, Moscow, Russia
- ⬊ Australian International School, Singapore
- ⬊ Beijing Huijia Private School, Beijing, China
- ⬊ International School of Kuala Lumpur, Kuala Lumpur, Malaysia
- ⬊ International School of Uganda, Kampala, Uganda
- ⬊ Kororoit Creek Primary School, Melbourne, Australia
- ⬊ Melbourne Grammar School, Melbourne, Australia
- ⬊ Neev Academy, Bangalore, India
- ⬊ Presbyterian Ladies College, Perth, Australia
- ⬊ Qatar Academy, Doha, Qatar
- ⬊ Ruyton Girls School, Melbourne, Australia
- ⬊ Shanghai Community International School, Shanghai, China
- ⬊ Stonehill International School, Bangalore, India
- ⬊ Waikowhai Intermediate School, Auckland, New Zealand
- ⬊ Wesley College, Melbourne, Australia

MORE FROM
ELEVATE BOOKS EDU

Dive into Inquiry: Amplify Learning and Empower Student Voice
By Trevor MacKenzie

Dive into Inquiry beautifully marries the voice and choice of inquiry with the structure and support required to optimize learning. With Dive into Inquiry, you'll gain an understanding of how to best support your learners as they shift from a traditional learning model into the inquiry classroom where student agency is fostered and celebrated each and every day.

Inquiry Mindset: Nurturing the Dreams, Wonders, and Curiosities of Our Youngest Learners
By Trevor MacKenzie and Rebecca Bushby

Inquiry Mindset offers a highly accessible journey through inquiry in the younger years. Learn how to empower your students, increase engagement, and accelerate learning by harnessing the power of curiosity. With practical examples and a step-by-step guide to inquiry, Trevor MacKenzie and Rebecca Bushby make inquiry-based learning simple.

Inquiry Mindset: Assessment Edition—Scaffolding a Partnership for Equity and Agency in Learning
By Trevor MacKenzie

Trevor takes another deep dive into inquiry as he examines the role of assessment in education through the lens of co-designing and co-constructing with students. In *Inquiry Mindset: Assessment Edition*, he outlines the beliefs, values, and frameworks that allow teachers to scaffold assessments infused with student voice, understanding, and autonomy.

Getting Personal with Inquiry Learning: Guiding Learners' Explorations of Personal Passions, Interests and Questions
By Kath Murdoch

In *Getting Personal with Inquiry Learning*, world-renowned inquiry expert, Kath Murdoch, draws on decades of experience to offer a thorough, practical guide to supporting young learners' investigations into their passions, interests, and questions. The book invites teachers to take their thinking about inquiry to the next level and to truly honor both their own and their students' agency.

From Agency to Zest: A Journey through the Landscape of Inquiry
By Kath Murdoch

Designed to be used to initiate reflection and to provoke professional dialogue amongst educators, *From Agency to Zest* offers insight into inquiry as an approach to teaching and learning. In addition to the explanations provided throughout, Murdoch offers practical advice on how to support and deepen professional learning experiences within and across schools.

Leading with a Lens of Inquiry: Cultivating Conditions for Curiousity and Emowering Agency
By Jessica Vance

Typical models of training and professional development focus on telling. It's a model that far too often trickles down to classrooms where the traditional way of "doing school" limits the way educators teach and students learn. Fortunately, there is a better way to learn: through wonder, agency, and inquiry. From *Leading with a Lens of Inquiry* administrators, educational instructors, and peer leaders learn how to cultivate learning spaces that ignite curiosity and inspire critical thinking in adult and student learners alike.

The AI Infused Classroom: Inspiring Ideas to Shift Teaching and Maximize Meaningful Learning in the World of AI
By Holly Clark

With the right mindset, the right questions, and the right strategies, you can use AI to create and broaden meaningful learning experiences for every student. In *The AI Infused Classroom*, Holly Clark points out that students need well-trained educators now more than ever, to ensure they are prepared for the world of AI. This book equips you to navigate the latest iteration of edtech.

The Google Infused Classroom: A Guidebook to Making Thinking Visible and Amplifying Student Voice
By Holly Clark and Tanya Avrith

This beautifully designed book offers guidance on using technology to design instruction that allows students to show their thinking, demonstrate their learning, and share their work (and voices!) with authentic audiences. *The Google Infused Classroom* will equip you to empower your students to use technology in meaningful ways that prepare them for the future.

The Microsoft Infused Classroom: A Guidebook to Making Thinking Visible and Amplifying Student Voice
By Holly Clark and Tanya Avrith

Packed with ideas you can use in your classroom tomorrow, *The Microsoft Infused Classroom*, Designed equips you to use powerful tools that put learning first. Edtech experts led by Holly Clark and Tanya Avrith show you how to use technology to increase engagement in your classroom and provide authentic opportunities for students to share their work and their voice.

The Chromebook Infused Classroom: Using Blended Learning to Create Engaging, Student-Centered Classrooms
By Holly Clark

Edtech expert and trainer Holly Clark serves as your guide to using Chromebooks effectively in the classroom. As with other books in the Infused Classroom series, *The Chromebook Infused Classroom* relies on proven pedagogical practices to create engaging and meaningful learning experiences for today's students. With its wealth of tools, ideas, and step-by-step instructions, this book equips you to empower your students for learning—and for life.

The HyperDoc Handbook: Digital Lesson Design Using Google Apps
By Lisa Highfill, Kelly Hilton, and Sarah Landis

The HyperDoc Handbook is a practical reference guide for all K–12 educators who want to transform their teaching into blended-learning environments. The HyperDoc Handbook is a bestselling book that strikes the perfect balance between pedagogy and how-to tips while also providing ready-to-use lesson plans to get you started with HyperDocs right away.

The InterACTIVE Classroom: Using Technology to Make Learning more Relevant and Engaging in the Elementary Classroom
By Joe and Kristin Merrill

In this practical and idea-packed book, coauthors, classroom teachers, and edtech experts Joe and Kristin Merrill share their personal framework for creating an interACTIVE classroom. You'll find new ways to inspire young learners to grow and to develop grit as they stretch their thinking and abilities.

Flipgrid in the InterACTIVE Class: Encouraging Inclusion and Student Voice in the Elementary
By Joe and Kristin Merrill

Classroom teachers Joe and Kristin Merrill have seen firsthand how the practical ideas shared in *Flipgrid in the InterACTIVE Class* impact learning. By equipping teachers to design more opportunities for students to share their voices and create more equitable learning experiences, Flipgrid opens the door for interaction and discussion in the elementary classroom.

Sketchnotes for Educators: 100 Inspiring Illustrations for Lifelong Learners
By Sylvia Duckworth

Sylvia Duckworth is a Canadian teacher whose sketchnotes have taken social media by storm. Her drawings provide clarity and provoke dialogue on many topics related to education. This book contains 100 of her most popular sketchnotes with links to the original downloads that can be used in class or shared with colleagues. Interspersed throughout the book are Sylvia's reflections on each drawing and what motivated her to create them, in addition to commentary from other educators who inspired the sketchnotes.

How to Sketchnote: Visual Note-taking Made Easy
By Sylvia Duckworth

Educator and internationally known sketchnoter Sylvia Duckworth makes ideas memorable and shareable with her simple yet powerful drawings. In *How to Sketchnote*, she explains how you can use sketchnoting in the classroom and that you don't have to be an artist to discover the benefits of doodling!

40 Ways to Inject Creativity into Your Classroom with Adobe Spark
By Ben Forta and Monica Burns

Experienced educators Ben Forta and Monica Burns offer step-by-step guidance on how to incorporate this powerful tool into your classroom in ways that are meaningful and relevant. They present 40 fun and practical lesson plans suitable for a variety of ages and subjects as well as 15 graphic organizers to get you started. With the tips, suggestions, and encouragement in this book, you'll find everything you need to inject creativity into your classroom using Adobe Spark.